"Alexei Parshchikov's 'I Lived on the Battlefield of Poltava' (1989), an import; cal poem imbued with parodic touches, sheds a new light on Pushkin's *Poltava* and its legacy. It challenges Pushkin's mythologised portrayal of the Great Northern War by presenting everyday life in late twentieth-century Poltava through the prism of palimpsestic imagination influenced by Russian cultural memory.

Donald Wesling's excellent translation of Parshchikov's 'I Lived on the Battlefield of Poltava' animates effectively the playful space created in the poem through the powerful use of metaphor, associative language and surreal overtones. Wesling shows an exceptional sensitivity to Parshchikov's exuberant language and renders the performance-like quality of the poem exquisitely. Parshchikov's concerns with the inevitability of change, the importance of place and the power of language to transform realities embedded in this poem make his version of the historical event—reimagined in a decolonising manner—highly appealing to the readers of the 2020s."

— Alexandra Smith, Reader in Russian Studies at the University of Edinburgh

"When Alexei Parshchikov, perhaps the greatest poet of the Russian *perestroika* generation, died prematurely in 2009, he could not know that Ukraine, where he had spent much of his childhood and youth, would one day rise up against its Soviet rulers. It was in the Battle of Poltava (1709), that Russia first seized control from Charles XII, the King of Sweden of the territory in question. Parshchikov's brilliant Poundian 'poem including history'—as well as geography and ecology—juxtaposes superbly surreal battle scenes with the quiet meditations of the poet, cultivating, on the site of the former battlefield, his garden, with its apricot trees, its 'long-nosed field mice' and 'fruit-honey grog,' and celebrating Ivan Mazepa, the Russian commander turned Ukrainian opposition fighter, and his sweetheart Marfa Kochubey. In Donald Wesling's excellent rhymed-verse translation, which dissolves into free rhythms in the course of the poem, Parschikov's brilliant and highly original imagination lives again. It could not be more apropos today!"

— Marjorie Perloff, author of *Infrathin: An Experiment in Micropoetics*

"One of great poetic achievements of the 1980s, Parshchikov's long poem appears, in Donald Wesling's ambitious new translation, startlingly of our time—not just because of its dismantling of Russian imperialist myths but also because of its insistence on the multifarious resilience of language in the face of its misuse and of the horrors of wars, past and present."

— Jacob Edmond, author of *Make It the Same: Poetry in the Age of Global Media*

"From the twelfth to the twenty-first century, Ukraine has been periodically destroyed by those who would own it. Among these blood-soaked backstories, the three-way struggle between Peter the Great, Sweden's Charles XII, and the treacherous Ukrainian Cossack Mazepa in 1709 has long been pan-European lore. In this 'historical-geographical-ecological' evocation by the Russian metarealist Alexei Parshchikov, the poet is tending his garden on the site of the battle. Knives, bits of cannon and bone, snatches of sexual violence and the Tsar's largesse emerge from the black earth. Sacrificial lambs and mosquitos look on. Donald Wesling's spectacular rendering into English, reflecting subtexts in Pushkin as well as the late Soviet poetic underground, is formally audacious and so tightly constructed that the reader can't breathe. Exactly what is required today."

— Caryl Emerson, Princeton University

I Lived on the Battlefield of Poltava

Alexei
Parshchikov

Cherry
Orchard
Books

I Lived on the Battlefield of Poltava

Alexei Parshchikov

Translated from the Russian
by **Donald Wesling**

BOSTON

2023

Library of Congress Cataloging-in-Publication Data

Names: Parshchikov, Alekseĭ, author. | Wesling, Donald, translator.
Title: I lived on the Battlefield of Poltava / Alexei Parshchikov; translated from the Russian by Donald Wesling.
Other titles: ÍA zhil na pole Poltavskoĭ bitvy. English
Description: Boston: Cherry Orchard Books, an imprint of Academic Studies Press, 2023.
Identifiers: LCCN 2023021388 (print) | LCCN 2023021389 (ebook) | ISBN 9798887192246 (hardback) | ISBN 9798887192253 (paperback) | ISBN 9798887192260 (adobe pdf) | ISBN 9798887192277 (epub)
Subjects: LCSH: Poltava, Battle of, Poltava, Ukraine, 1709--Poetry. | LCGFT: Historical poetry. | Poetry.
Classification: LCC PG3485.A735 I3913 2023 (print) | LCC PG3485.A735 (ebook) | DDC 891.71/44--dc23/eng/20230512

LC record available at https://lccn.loc.gov/2023021388
LC ebook record available at https://lccn.loc.gov/2023021389

ISBN 9798887192246 (hardback)
ISBN 9798887192253 (paperback)
ISBN 9798887192260 (adobe pdf)
ISBN 9798887192277 (epub)

Book design by Kryon Publishing Services.
Cover design by Ivan Grave.

Published by Cherry Orchard Books, an imprint of Academic Studies Press
1577 Beacon Street
Brookline, MA 02446, USA
press@academicstudiespress.com
www.academicstudiespress.com

This 2023 translation
is dedicated to
Ekaterina Drobyazko,
Alexei Parshchikov's
widow, with thanks
for her efforts to keep
his writing alive and
available for readers.

Содержание

Contents

From the Translator

Alexei Parshchikov (b. 1954 in Olga in the Russian Far East) was a writer in the Russian language, but lived his early years and many later years in Ukraine. He studied agriculture in college. In the 1980s he was member of several avant-garde groups in Moscow, associated for instance with the fantastical dissident Dmitri Prigov, and he worked with Arkadii Dragomoshchenko and Club 81 in what was then Leningrad. In the 1990s he left Russia for good and spent two years earning a degree at Stanford University, where his thesis was on Prigov. During this stint in California, he visited me in San Diego and we drove inland from the coast to the Anza Borrego desert, along with my UC San Diego class of writers. At the desert he loved the non-human scale, the entire want of vegetation. After his return to Europe, I lost touch with him, but here in my note are precious late-life facts.[1]

I first knew Parshchikov in Moscow and Kyiv in the late 1980s. In Moscow he introduced me to Dmitri Prigov, Ilya Kutik, and Mikhail Epshtein. He was my guide in Kyiv for a week in autumn 1988, where he introduced me to writers, journalists, singers, and architectural and religious sites. He was in

---

1   Ekaterina Drobyazko, the poet's widow, wrote to me in March 2023: "After Stanford, Parshchikov lived for a short time with his wife Martina Hügli. They separated, and in 1996 he joined his parents in exile in Germany. Since the late 90s, Parshchikov continued to travel to poetry festivals: for example, to Rotterdam, and to readings in Moscow. He translated from English the book *Sun* by Michael Palmer (2000), and participated in Vyborg, a project by Finnish-American artist Lisa Roberts (2001) . . . We got married in 2002 . . . [Also in] 2002 there appeared under one cover *Metarealist Poets*, with poems by AP, Alexander Eremenko, and Ivan Zhdanov. In subsequent years, Alyosha published books in Moscow: *Soprikosnovenie pauz* (2004), the poems and essays in *Angary* (2006), *Rai medlennogo ognia* (2006), and *Zemletriasenie v bukhte Ze* (2008). The latest initiative of Alyosha was the translation, together with Patrick Henry and Mark Shatunovsky, of American poet Charles Bernstein's *Artifice of Absorption* (2008). [I should add that] in 2005 he met [the] German poet/translator Hendrik Jackson and began translating his poetry and essays. He was the initiator [of bringing] modern German poets to the Moscow Biennale of Poets in 2005, where he himself won the award in the category 'Literary Legend.' Our son Matthäus was born in 2006. In the same year, Alyosha had his first operation. The second was in 2008. Alyosha died in Cologne on April 3, 2009. He was buried in the ancient city cemetery [called] Melaten."

Leningrad at the time of the 1988 reading by Robert Creeley in a palace on Nevsky Prospekt, and took part in hosting the American writer. The cover of this book is a photo I took at the time. It is placed here as a record of Alexei at a moment just before the 1989 publication of his wonderful book *Figures of Intuition*, which contains the *poema*, or long poem, titled *I Lived on the Battlefield of Poltava*. In the 1989 volume, most of the poem is printed sideways to accommodate the long lines.[2]

Official publishing houses in Russia before the fall of communism in 1989 were publishing books that seem, in retrospect, astonishingly innovative, complex in theme and treatment, avant-garde, and personal. What we may have missed about the period was that new work coexisted with official and socially approved writing by Writers' Union members; the new poets were not Union members, but had lunch privileges (and could run lectures and readings) in the grand sanctuaries of the official writers with their ten-foot statues of Mayakovsky. The actual published volumes of the new poets were pamphlet-like, small in size and with tiny print fonts, and sold for a few rubles, but their contents pushed against every boundary except the one involving the viability of the Russian political system: there, there only, did censorship draw the line. Writers were exquisitely sensitive to that line and so able to test it. Since then, of course, almost everything has changed.

This is a poem historical-geographical-ecological. It plays upon/against a name that readers in the West may not fully appreciate, though in our time, after the very recent Russian invasion of Crimea, the Donbas, and now the whole independent country of Ukraine, the question about the name is a terrible thing to those living in the region. Ukraine, U-Kraina, literally means "On the Border," and so the historical issue is sedimented in the term for the nation. (Parshchikov in his long poem alludes to this issue by speaking more than once of "the country called U.") Ukrainians cannot escape their anguish-of-relation to Russia because it is deep-buried in the consciousness of their language, and because it has existential force in their history. Russian autocrats who owned them as a Russian republic until 1989 still feel Ukraine is within their sphere because it is on their immediate margin and was theirs

---

2 *Figures of Intuition*, Russian title *Figury intuitsii*, was published by Moskovskii rabochii in Moscow in 1989. The poem can be found there on pages 31–69. It is of some interest that the book is a quarter inch thick, five by six inches in flat dimensions, and cost thirty-five kopecks. The title page of my copy of this book has this inscription: "for Donald / even in the desert we feel ourselves together with the poetry, and the desert appreciates it / Alexei Parshchikov / Ca. 1991." The more recent edition of the Poltava poem, which became the basis of this translation, is to be found in Alexei Parshchikov, *Dirizhabli* [Dirigibles], with an introduction by Ilya Kukulin (Moscow: Vremia, 2014), 68–94.

until recently. Historically, they won Ukraine at the Battle of Poltava in 1709 even though the name of the territory came later. For Russians, the flashpoint is that Ukraine in its new status, and with its own language and political system, could be drawn westward through membership in NATO.

In the poem, the players are Charles XII of Sweden, who was far from home with his regiments when he was defeated (and shot in the foot!) at the Battle of Poltava, though this did not stop his dynastic ambitions for new territory; Peter the Great in St. Petersburg, whose generals brought up troops and cannon to defeat the invader of lands that he claimed as his own; and Ivan Mazepa, the treacherous Hetman of the Zaporozhtsy Cossacks on both banks of the Dnipro. As traitor to Peter and Russia, Mazepa aligned with the Swedish king in order to rule the territory that his ethnic minority already occupied. The historical ambiguity, still an issue in Ukraine and in this poem, is that Mazepa is by one reading a Ukrainian patriot, and by another the betrayer who sent his forces to fight for Russia. After all, Russia is forever the victor in that battle. (Four times more Swedes died in the battle than Russians, and Russia's rule was solidified until the undoing of communism centuries later, just a few years after the time of writing of this poem, which ironically is not in the Ukrainian but in the Russian language.) There is also Mariya Kochubey, nicknamed Marfa, the hetman's goddaughter: is she a sex-object and a punchingbag for Mazepa, or is that the author's invention? (Being a godfather was, and still is, a serious religious obligation in the Orthodox Church, so what is happening in chapter two may be blasphemy as well as sexual violence.)

The other actors are the soldiers on both sides, whose lives were lost, blood soaked into the black Ukrainian soil just where the writer is tending his garden. For the dynasts the writer has ironic scorn; for the soldiers nothing but fellow-feeling, respect, pity. Chapter one concerns the origins of cannon and knives, a deep dive into the human need to harm enemy others. These are fantasy-origins, but the energies of disgust are real in the poem's language.

A poem, then, that contains history, and that interrogates it. History: overlay and interpenetration of eras. Eras widely separated in time, but their location is the same, a stretch of ground where men of different nations, under different flags, fight and die. The ground is sacred, even though now it is covered with train-tracks and a psychiatric hospital, and the writer's plot of earth where he observes plants and animals, tends his garden, relaxes in his hammock, drinks the local grog, works in a nearby bar, meets a young woman who is a modern girl but sometimes fades into the imaginary image of historical Marfa.

Ecology, too. Parshchikov's training as agronomist is evident everywhere in the poem. It can be traced in his frequent use of names of animals and plants, in the practical notice of work on the land, and in concern for the lives and deaths of non-human beings including an ant and beetles of several species. He also loves and uses place names, including those of the local river and forest, as well as nearby towns. In one section, Parshchikov speaks as a little lamb, entering the consciousness of the animal other, an animal as a potential victim of our weapons. He saves for his last action, and the near-to-last use of personal pronouns for himself, an account of spraying his territory with blue vitriol. He is himself poisoning the living beings in the surroundings, but also by extension making dead once again the historical and geographical actors of the previous sections. The garden is what has obliterated the battlefield by action of time and growth.

Chapter two, part seven is the most famous section in the poem, rightly so for its picture of devastation of everything including the narrator and the human as a war-making species. Whisk it all away! This long-line section is the culmination of the long poem, the best thing in the *poema*, and one of the great examples of garden poetry in world literature (the best since Andrew Marvell's "The Garden" in the seventeenth century, and more capacious than Marvell because of the historical contempt it carries). The author's point: Now we're killers even of the gardens where we once found solace and recreation and pleasure, so gardens are no longer the classic opposite, to play off against battlefields. Blue vitriol is the indissoluble evil in our blood and bones. The agronomist/ecologist is also a thinker because he is also a killer.[3]

The previous translations from this long poem are in flexible free verse, which is entirely appropriate for this writer.[4] These do well to capture the interruptive logic of the original, the line of broken-

3 An early recognition of Parshchikov's long poem for the English-speaking world, and the best interpretation I know, is in Alexandra Smith's *Montaging Pushkin: Pushkin and Visions of Modernity in Russian Twentieth-Century Poetry* (Amsterdam and New York: Rodopi Editions, 2006). Alexandra Smith calls this long poem "perhaps the most important achievement of Russian post-perestroika poetry" (ibid., 318). She notes that the poem was the winner of the Andrei Bely Prize in 1985. Ilya Kukulin also remarks on the poem in his introduction to *Dirigibles*.

4 There are translations of single sections of the whole poem in John High et al., eds., *Crossing Centuries: The New Generation in Russian Poetry* (Jersey City, NJ: Talisman House, 2000); and in Alexei Parshchikov, *Blue Vitriol*, a selection of the major poems including part of the Poltava, with translations by John High, Michael Molnar, and Michael Palmer, and an introduction by Marjorie Perloff (Pengrove, CA: Avec Books, 1994). Not from this long poem, but with

off speech and of quick-change images that makes Parshchikov's Russian so vivid as personal style. Because this has already been achieved for the introduction and for the blue vitriol section of the text, and already valid, I have chosen instead to *follow the original* in its decision that most of the poem, in the first two chapters (before the quirky prose of chapter three), should be in traditional rhyme and meter. The poem is wildly various and imaginative in its thinking and its welling-up of images in sequences, but it is carefully Pushkinian in its outer forms. That disjunction is intentional and artistic, and cannot be achieved, at least in a similar way, in American free verse. Also, as a matter of scale, here we have the whole poem in its clever turnings. I have tried to give the equivalents for that complex feeling-tone in English, and it has involved imitating the way the rhyming is very often opportunistic and an occasion for humor through sound effects. Also, I have sometimes added elements in part-lines so as to be more explicit than the original: this to help the reader better understand the allusions and meanings of the original Russian. The notes at the end also aim at unobtrusive clarification. I will add that there are many leaping forms of logic and unexpected metaphors, in the Russian and therefore in the translation, that should not be clarified. These are to be respected and interrogated, as Alexei Parshchikov's signature innovations in style. In the introduction he himself says it all: "this jumping method of movement."

Briefly, to focus the interpretation of the poem's structures of meaning, large and small, I would double back to its late-Soviet origin in the mid-1980s; the time when Mikhail Epshtein invented for this writer and two others the name "metarealists." After 1989, Alexei Parshchikov would say that his grouping in a school of metarealism with Ivan Zhdanov and Aleksandr Eremenko was inexact, even mythical. However, without doubt, his friend Epshtein's brilliant campaign helped the visibility of all three unofficial writers as somewhat similar, especially in their attitudes toward pre-1989 Soviet conventional thinking, and toward metaphors in poems. Here, bringing to the Poltava poem a topic of some contention, I would pull out a couple of strands from existing definitions of 1980s metarealism. (Note, for context, that before 1989, in the death-throes of communism, these writers hovered in discomfort between an unofficial and an official existence, but at least they had an audience. After 1989, most of them lost an audience and a mission along with a national identity, as the door they were kick-

---

fine versions of stand-alone poems, the other translations known to me are in Kent Johnson and Stephen M. Ashby, eds., *Third Wave: The New Russian Poetry* (Ann Arbor: University of Michigan Press, 1992); and in Alexei Parshchikov, *Selected Poems*, trans. Michael Palmer and Wayne Chambliss (New York: KRik Publishing House, 2016).

ing was suddenly flung open. What they then had left was the Russian language, and the assignment of what to do with new freedoms.)

The poetics of metarealism involved questioning culturally established meanings. They foregrounded the fluidity of meaning, the perception of a world where one reality hides another, the values of incongruity and unexpectedness. In poetic practice, this meant reacting to a disturbed existence, a stubbornly thing-like reality that opens up beyond the metaphor, with yet a heavy emphasis on this device as both literal and figurative. For metaphor as both a local device and a larger structure, these poetics took the prefix "co-" of ideological *comparison* as more urgent than any "meta-" of *likening*. If I relate this 1980s social poetics to Poltava as a historical poem of the late-Soviet underground, I find these multi-planar associations-in-contrast: a heroic official battleground *with* a vegetable garden on the same site in present-day Ukraine; a gardener who kills every living thing in his plot with blue vitriol; a dolphin who drives a car in the landlocked middle of a continent; a speaking lamb; and an introduction and two chapters in strict traditional verse, skillfully handled, *with* a third and final chapter in sentences-equal-to-line, stabbing free verse.[5]

***

Since a college course with Hugh McLean on Russian fiction, I have worked to learn the Russian language through native-speaker tutors, two summer-long workshops, computer courses through Rosetta Stone, and three months in then-Leningrad on a fellowship at Leningrad State University to confer on poetry with German Vasilievich Filippov. I managed to require glasses for the first time, in my forties, working with Russian dictionaries. I met with scholars at conferences on Russian thinker

---

5   Books and articles exist that pursue the history of the metarealist school, and that try defining key terms. The main articles and books by Mikhail Epshtein, the 1980s inventor of metarealism as a style, are listed in the bibliography of Aleksandr Zhitenev, whose recent article on "The Circle of Metarealist Poets" appears in *The Oxford Book of Soviet Underground Culture*, ed. Mark Lipovetsky et al. (Oxford: Oxford University Press, 2021). I also recommend Zhitenev's clever and comprehensive article, and the book by Ol'ga Severskaia, *Iazyk poeticheskoi shkoly: idiolekt, idiostil', sotsiolekt* (Moscow: Rossiskaia akademiia nauk, Institut russkogo iazyka im. V. V. Vinogradova, 2007). I will mention that I devote a few close-reading pages to Parshchikov's metarealist lyric, "Minus-Korabl" [Minus Ship] (1980s), in my book *Animal Perception and Literary Language* (New York: Palgrave Macmillan, 2019). I will mention that I devote a few close-reading pages to Parshchikov's metarealist lyric, "Minus-Korabl" [Minus Ship] (1980s), in my book *Animal Perception and Literary Language* (New York: Palgrave Macmillan, 2019).

Mikhail Bakhtin and wrote a book on *Bakhtin and the Social Moorings of Poetry* (Lewisburg, PA: Bucknell University Press, 2004). At that time, I was one of many persons who received the immense intellectual generosity of the famous Russianist Caryl Emerson. With that as preparation, I have found extremely helpful an English prose version by Slav Tsarynnyk, who set the poem up in lines and in strict Russian word-order. When, here, the syntax in English seems peculiar, most often that is the Russian syntax shining through the sentence. When the notes are factual they are by Slav Tsarynnyk; when the notes are interpretive they are by me. The author's brief footnotes appear at the end of the Russian text of the poem, and all five of these are further explained in my notes at the end of the translation.

Donald Wesling
Pacific Beach, California

Я жил на поле Полтавской Битвы

п о э м а

Алексей Парщиков

I Lived on the Battlefield of Poltava

Alexei Parshchikov

Translated from the Russian by
Donald Wesling

Вступление

Беги, моя строчка, мой пёс — лови! — и возвращайся к ноге
с веткой в сходящихся челюстях, и снова служи дуге, —

улетает посылка глазу на радость, а мышцам твоим на работу,
море беру и метаю — куда? — и море приспосабливается к полёту,

уменьшаясь, как тень от очков в жгучий день, когда их на пробу
приближают к лицу, и твердея, как эта же тень, только чтобы

лечь меж бумагой и шрифтом и волниться во рту языком; наконец,
вспышка! — и расширяется прежнее море, но за срезом страниц.

Буквы, вы — армия, ослепшая вдруг и бредущая краем времён,
мы вас видим вплотную — рис ресниц, и сверху — риски колонн, —

брошена техника, люди, как на кукане, связаны температурой тел,
но очнутся войска, доберись хоть один до двенадцатислойных стен

Идеального Города, и выпись на чистом, и стань — херувим,
новым зреньем обводит нас текст и от лиц наших не отделим.

Всё, что я вижу, вилку даёт от хрусталика — в сердце и мозг,
и, скрестившись на кончиках пальцев, ссыпается в лязг

Introduction

Run out, my line, my dog—and catch!—run back to my foot,[1]
Branch in your closing jaws, complete the arc of throw, then out

Away again it sails, work for your muscles, joy for your eyes,
Then I scoop the sea and toss it—where?—sea entire flies,

Reduces in size to a sunglass lens, bright day, lift
These frames to face, the lens light hardens, the shadow will shift

To lay sense between paper and print, make waves with the tongue; last,
Return that previous sea but now with the pages surpassed,

Flash! Letters, you—you alphabet army now blind,
Eye-lash brush-stroke—you columns drawn along the edge of time,

Abandoned equipment, packs of men like fish strung
Blood-cold on a line,[2] but these troops wake, attack along

The Perfect City's walls, sleep on clean floors, each then
Is!—clear-eye cherub of my text, their faces mine.

All things I see will fractal-in from eye to heart, around
The brain, then exit tips of fingers, now the sound

машинописи; вот машинка — амфитеатр, спиной развёрнутый к хору,
лист идёт, как лавина бы — вспять! вбок — поправка — и в гору.

Выиграй, мой инструмент, кинь на пальцах — очко! — а под углом
иным — те же буквы летят, словно комья земли, и лепится холм,

чуть станина дрожит, и блестят рычажки в капельках масла,
а над ними — не раскрытые видом гребешки душистые смысла,

сам не лёгок я на подъём, больше сил против лени затрачу,
а в машинку заложены кипы полётов и способ движенья прыгучий!

Правь на юг, с изворотом, чтоб цокнули мы языком над Стокгольмом,
уцепившись за клавишу — Ъ — мы оставим первопрестольный

снег. Я обольщён жарой. Север спокоен, как на ботинке узел, —
тем глубже он занят собой, чем резче ты дёрнешь морозный усик.

Не в благоденствии дело, но чтоб дух прокормить, соберём травы,
на хуторах плодоносных петляя в окрестностях тёплой Полтавы,

вот я, Господи, весь, вот мой пёс, он бежит моей властью
васильками — Велеса внук — и возвращается — св. Власий.

Of my typewriter: here, machine, the chorus of keys can mount
Where the white sheet comes avalanching down the cirque, up then in front.

Play it, my instrument, splay fingers—point!—new view—
Same letters bounce, earth clods build up into a queue.

It slightly trembles on its base, oil droplets glitter
On moving levers, while on top there's scent of subject matter,

I myself not always ready for anything, use too much force versus
My laziness, pull reams of flights through my machine, make verses

From this jumping method of movement! So! switch south to Stockholm,
Keep typing Russian's hard-sign key,[3] tongue-clicks unspoken,

Snow's left behind. I love this heat. Back north: calm; like a knot
In a boot-lace, you pull its tendril, it gets obstinate.

My topic isn't wealth but health, to feed our spirits rather,
By gathering herbs from villages surrounding warm Poltava.

And here I am, my God, all here—my dog, runs by my powers,
A god of earth and saint of church[4]—runs back through the cornflowers.

Глава первая,
в которой повествуется о происхождении оружия

1.1

Где точка опоры? Не по учебнику помню: галактики контур остист,
где точка опоры? Ушедший в воронку, чем кончится гаснущий свист?

Или перед собой её держит к забору теснящийся пыльный бурунчик,
или на донце сознания носит её трясогузка — прыткий стаканчик?

Но уронится заверть в расцепе с небесной зубчаткой, а птичка
вдоль отмели прыг-скок и ушла … Надо мной ли висит эта точка?

В сравнении с ней элементы восьмого периода — пух, дирижабли,
так тяжела эта точка и неустойчива — лишь время её окружает,

лишь ошмётки вселенной и палочки-души (две-три), прежде чем
утратиться вовсе, край иглы озирают, и — нет глубже ям.

Словно газета, заглавьем читая концовку, вращаясь и рея,
ближе к точке кривляются все, — кто же мог быть смешон перед нею?

Chapter One,
Which Tells about the Origin of Weapons

1.1

What base[5] will bear us up? The galaxy, books say,
Is spiny, what base there? Will some vortex suck us away?

Perhaps the point of support's some dusty field's far track,
Perhaps essential mind rides on a wagtail's[6] back,

Or ripped from heaven's wheel, sent out the vortex
To vanish like that bird, fly sky-high unsupported?

The lightness of feathery fluff, or of dirigibles,
Contrasts the gravity of battlefields when time's divisible.

The universe distils itself and makes a weapon,
Blam-blam, and then retracts itself, goes black-hole deep.

I read the newspaper heading which contains its ending,
No spinning it, no grimacing, all jokes suspended.

От неё отделяются гладкие мелкие камушки — их пустота облизала —
это души оружия, и сразу становится тесно в штабах и казармах.

Обнаружились души оружия, намечаясь в эфире, как только
в лоск притёрлись приклады к ладоням, в идее — обычная галька.

Меж людьми побродила винтовка и знает, что такое удар по улыбке,
застилая полвоздуха, пуля из-под ног извергает булыжник.

Ах, чем палить по мишеням новобранцами ада, лучше пить в одиночку!
Хмельное тело затылком нащупывает самовитую точку.

Она свободней, чем оборванный трос, чертящий на воздухе лепестки,
гуляет — где хочет, и в неё никогда не прицеливаются стрелки.

Это точка опоры галактики — не вершина, а низ блаженства,
от неё и пушка и нож, их морозное совершенство.

Smooth pebbles, loved by emptiness, detach their mass
From time-space: souls of weapons, heaped here from the past.

Field pebbles now appear as souls of guns. In thought
Already we're adjusting our hands to their airy butts.[7]

Among our crowd a rifle wanders; and a foolish
Smile flickers when boulders obscure the air, blown up by bullets.

Ah, fresh recruits from Sweden-Russia fire hic et nunc,
Farm boys zetz-slapped upside the occiput, killed drunk.

The point of support, free as a loose rope, she for short,
Will wander where she wants, un-aimed-at and unshot.

Our galaxy comes straight from her,[8] this bliss of dejection
In this ecology of cannon and knife in their frozen perfection.

1.2. Первая пушка

Первая пушка была рассчитана на любопытство врага
и число частей её — по числу врагов.
На левом берегу Ворсклы возвели водяные меха,
а между ними — колонну со скобкой для рычагов,
по краям которых подцеплены широкие платформы.
В ботфортах, заказанных для данного офорта,
люди вереницей шли с платформы на платформу

и обратно,

такие весы поочерёдно давили на меха,
получался массовый насос, выталкивающий два заряда
и дающий общее распеделение греха.
Меха и колонна покоились на шестиколёсном помосте,
а вдоль реки пробегала кожаная кишка,
надуваясь от насоса, она гнала колёса и вместе
всех артиллеристов, удивлённых слегка[1].

* * *

Копиисты писали машину на облаке, палящую лагом,
в этом был урок мореходного и авиа-духа,
и косила врага, как вертлюг разболтанная костомаха,
колёса за её спиной напоминали два уха.
Пушка могла быть разобрана на мельчайшие частички
и разнесена по свету в нагрудных карманах армий,
спрятана за щеками или вплетена в косички
и т.п., что ещё не перенято нами.

* * *

1.2. The First Cannon

First cannon designed curious enemy in mind
Number of moving levers same number life-leavers
Left bank Vorskla[9] Russian fellows built water bellows
Spaced out high scaffolds each attach massive brackets
Each bracket push-down planks holding up-down plankforms
In thick boots commissioned for this route
Bank villagers single file walk up-back forms the while
Press down bellows alternate with their villager weight
A pump collecting massive force for massive release
A force-pump within releasing an even distribution of sin.
Bellows and plankforms raised on massy six-wheeled chassis
And strung along river rivage a long and leather sausage
Air-inflated by the pump wheels revolve and gunners jump
Killers themselves though battle-wise themselves slightly surprised.[10]

*　*　*

Abstract force and loud power machinery air and cloud
Threat to head-aim things fish fins and bird wings
Mow down frontal shatter by burst swivel of osseous matter.
Huge wheels behind this engine's back looked like
Two ears. The cannon could be broken down
Into the smallest pieces and dispersed
Throughout the world in soldiers' pockets, packs,
Or hidden in their hair or cheeks, and so on.
Now we kill better, but they did masskill first.

*　*　*

Представим, что враг стоит напротив ствола.
Выстрел! — стрела соединяет грудь и спину,
тело руками обхватывает бесконечную машину,
тщится, становясь меньшим узлом большего узла.

* * *

И немедленно выравниваются весовые качели,
а тот солдат, что составил перевес,
взлетает, как завитушка мадонны Ботичелли,
и уходит за Малобудищанский лес.

И спалили конструкцию, в дыму не увидев ни зги.
Кто знал, что паровоз эту тьму растревожит?
«У него, — писал Маркс, — было в сущности две ноги,
которые он попеременно поднимал, как лошадь»[2].

Pretend your enemy's across the table
Shot! Arrow bolt hits chest and exits shoulder.
Foe's in the infinite machine, hands scrabble,
Small knot inside a big one growing colder.

* * *

Cannon sent bolts nails evening-out weighting scales
Man who caused the overweight up in air flies straight
Flies like a lock of hair on a botticelli madonna
And comes to rest in Mali Budyschcha forest.[11]

This closes in increasing blur, in smoke of history where
Is the locomotive can blast links through to eras past.
"He," Karl Marx wrote of tricky links, "Had in essence two legs
Which he lifted up alternately like a donkey."[12]

1.3. Ягнёнок рассказывает о распре двух братьев, которые пытались поймать его для жертвоприношения, и о том, как родился нож

Казалось, неба поперёк
шли ординарные скоты,
крутя ухмылками хвосты,
и чаяли уснуть. Пастух
меж них похож на поплавок,
нанизанный на чистый дух.

Варилась тонна комарья
и каждая из единиц
мир обегала вдоль границ,
их сумма жгла пружиной шерсть,
мне было больно. Думал я:
есть ангел и контрангел есть,

чьи чёрно-белые ряды,
как в упаковке для яиц,
и с точки зрения овец
они выносливее всех
и неделимы. Завиты
галактики — их яркий мех.

1.3. The Lamb Tells
about the Feud of Two Brothers,
Who Attempted to Catch Him
for Sacrificing,
and about How a Knife was Born

In my lamb eye, it seemed, there wrote
Across the sky some cows and stirks
Who twirled their tails in scowls and smirks,
Prepared to sleep. Between these cows bob-bobbled
A Shepherd like a fishing-float
Who seemed all conscience-clean and noble.

Mosquitos breeding-brewing weighed
A ton: each tiny, but alarming
When ZZZing down the steppe in swarming
Clouds, biting-burning lamby fur.
This hurt me. I thought things as I played:
Are angels and counter-angels are.

Oneinanother black and white,
An angel and an anti sleep
Egg-carton-like, so thinks a sheep.
Together opposite forever
In interference, they don't fight,
But like the galaxy dissever.

Я убегал от них, родных,
в скачке мой пыл — угольник сил,
в скачке я сахаром застыл,
растаял и возник, паря,
я знал, что изо всех моих
ног не получится ружья.

Бег, из чего была земля?
как два рельефа на одной
стене, они гнались стеной
за мной, о, их синхронный рёв
проснувшихся в крапиве. Я
расслабился в тени врагов.

За степью пролегал каньон:
скала, обрыв, скала, обрыв.
На скалах жил десяток трав,
висел на бурых корешках
травинок в пропастях озон
в каких-то призрачных мешках.

Из-за луны и мимо нас
катился весь в слезах клубок
простых колючек. Я залёг.
Они — искать! От сих до сих.
Но друг на друге взгляд увяз
преследователей моих.

Those two were shepherd brothers who
I was escaping by side-jumps.
My will solidified like lumps
Of melted sugar. I'm leaping stiffly
Because my leg, I somehow knew,
They'd make into a shot-gun rifle.

I'm running and what's the surround I see?
They're chasing me between two walls,
I run a tunnel where their calls
Coordinated tranquilize
Like stinging nettles. O. Shocked. I
Relax. Those foes' shouts paralyze.

Beyond the steppe the canyonlands:
Cliff, precipice, cliff, precipice.
And growing on those cliffs was Piss-
En-Lit, nine other herbs—and shoots
Of grasses with translucent glands
Of ozone hung from amber roots.

From 1 behind the moon and 2
Past us and 3 all covered-over
In tears, a ball of thorns came rolling.
I—slump! They—search! Here—there! Then—But!
These angry shepherd brothers[13] who'd
Chase me gazed each at each—at me not.

Открылся чудный разворот
земных осей, я заскользил
вдоль смерти, словно вдоль перил
в зоосаду вокруг оград,
где спал сверхслива-бегемот
и сливу ел под смех солдат.

Масштаб менялся наугад.
Мой Боже, ты не есть часы.
Я есмь не для колбасы,
история — не след во мглу.
Зачем вцепился в брата брат.
дай им двуручную пилу!

Сближаются. Взаимен слух.
И шаг. Мерцают кулаки.
Как проволочные мотки,
концы друг в друге ищут. Вящ
удар был брата брату в пах,
вспых! — над вознёй взлетела вещь.

Та вещь была разделена
в пропорции, примерно, пять
к двум, что поменьше — рукоять,
побольше — лезвие; соврёшь,
сказав: длина, ещё длина…
Спина подсказывает: нож,

Invaginated earth then opened
A wonderful unfold. I slipped
Along my death as if I'm strapped
To a greasy fence-rail in the zoo
And passing sleeping sugarplum hippos,
I ate a plum and started laughter in the troops.

Re-frame. Change scale and unpredict.
My God, lamb-God, you're outside time.
Don't kill me for kielbasa, I'm
Historical. Clear days. I'm still
Alive when Cain's blunt sickle pricks
Bro-holes in Abel. Hope: to kill.

The coming near. And then they hear
Each other. Then the fists are flashing
Like cut free coils of wire thrashing
Their dangerous loose ends. One
Brother strikes his brother there,
Flare! A thing pushed up that stabbed his groin.

That thing was built by means of ratios,
One part was five the other two.
What's smaller is the hilt—below;
What's larger—blade. You'd lose your life
If longer-longer's what you chose
Whose full length speaks the name of: knife,

ножа, ножу ножом, ноже.
В проёме занавеса клин
так разбегается в экран,
как нож обнял бы небеса.
Он здесь, и — нет его уже.
Но это принцип колеса.
Вслед за блуждающим ножом
уходит человек-магнит.
Нож! оглянись! Моих копыт
раздвоенных печать в кружке
Земли.
     Ночь.
         Воздух пережжён.
Душа на подкидной доске.

Knife's knives, to knife, by knife, O knife.
The curtain of your skin
Sustains a chink when knife goes in.
It's like the knife would unreveal.
It's like a seen-unseen downshift.
Reversal: principle of the wheel.
The wandering knives are drawn to us,
Their human magnet. Now they leave.
Knife! Get you gone! My bi-split hooves
Print circles in the battlefield
Of Earth.
    Night.
        The upper air's concussed.
Soul's up, soul's down, soul's heaven-helld.

1.4. Первое деловое отступление, Написанное в моём саду, расположенном на поле Полтавской битвы

Ребёнки — зайцеобразны: снизу два зуба, а щёки! Так же и зайцы —

детоподобны.

Злобны зайцы и непредсказуемы, словно осколки серы чиркнувшей спички.
Впереди мотоцикла и сзади — прыг-скок! — живые кавычки!
После октябрьских праздников по вечерам они сигают в мой сад,
наисмелейший проводку перегрызает и, сам чернея, отключает

свет.

Я ж защищаю саженец северного синапа от их аппетита
в одиночестве полном, где нету иллюзий единства и авторитета,
и сколько-то старых привычек не противоречат всякой новой привычке.
Я покупаю в хозмаге мешок мышеловок — розовые дощечки
с железным креплением, как сандалия Ахиллеса — где пятка
мифологическая, там у меня для приманки насажен колбасный

кружок.

А на заре обхожу мышеловки — попадаются бабочки и полёвки
и неизвестного вида зверьки типа гармошки в роговой окантовке.
Всем грызунам я горло перерезаю и вешаю их над ведром

головой вниз,

чтобы добыть множитель косоухого страха — кровь крыс.

Скисшую кровь я известью осветляю и побелочной щёткой
мажу остовы и скелетные ветви погуще, так, чтоб стекало с коры.
В сумерках заячье стадо вкруг сада лежит, являя сомнений бугры, —

1.4. The First Business Retreat, Written in My Garden, Located on the Field of the Poltava Battle

The children—like hares: two teeth on the bottom, just like hares—
                                                                    childlike.
Hares vicious, unpredictable, like shards of sulfur from the match I strike.
Like commas in front of my motorcycle, and behind—leap-jump! hares romp,
And, evenings after the October holidays,[14] here they are to chomp
My garden. These brave boys gnaw the hot-grid wires, house loses
                                                                    lights.
In autumn I keep Northern Synap apples from their appetites.
With them it's instinct, hunger, drive to survive, but it's not conscious malice.
With me it's habit; I kill little neighbors to protect my country palace.
I buy in the hardware store a bag of mousetraps—boards of pink
With metal bindings like Achilles' sandals—where Greeks would think
The heel is, there for bait I have a kielbasa sausage
                                                                    slice.
At dawn I walk around the traps—caught butterflies and caught field mice,
And animals of unlike species looking like accordions.
To rodents—cut their throats, string up, drip in buckets with
                                                                    heads down.
And multiplying the hares' fears of species-crossing, I saved rat's blood.

I mixed wet blood with dry slaked lime, got whitewash brush, so that I could
Paint tree trunks and bare branches thickly, soaking-dripping lethal bark.
At dusk the hares, in herds, with ears the shape of scissors, remain outside

да! — ни один из них не пойдёт хоть за билет в новый Ноев ковчег
через ограду: столь щепетилен и подавлен мой враг.
Ножницы-уши подняли и плачут, а я
                                                в жизни не видел зайца и крысу в обнимку!

Я же падаю в кресло-качалку листать руководство по садоводству,
днём тепло ещё и ужи — змеями здесь их не называют —
миллионы км проползают под солнцем, не сходя с места,
вот они на пригорке царят и, когда я их вижу, внезапно,
словно чулок ледяной мне надевают — это хвощёвое чувство.
Ух! Книгу читать, думать или вспоминать, а я выбираю — смотреть!
Сразу я забываю зайцев осадных и яблоню,
                                                я забываю того, кого вижу.

Что это в небе трепещет леса повыше и солнца пониже?

В этом краю, где женщины до облаков и прозрачны,
зрю ли я позвонок, что напротив пупа, и золотое меж них расстояние,
линию, нить, на какой раздувается жизнь на хромосомах,
как на прищепках — X, Y... Вдруг отстегнётся и по земле
                                                волочится
краем, как пододеяльник пустой, психика чья-то — на то воля Господня.
Там образуются души и бегут в дождевиках, как стрекозах —
мальчишка-кислород и девочка-глюкоза.

My garden fence. Yes! outside. Not for a ticket to New Noah's Ark
Would they come in. They're meek, meticulous against their suicide.
Hares cry ears up. I never
                    see hares hug a rat, companionate.

I fall into the rocking chair while flipping through the gardening manual.
Warm afternoons and grass-snakes—snakes they are not called in old Poltava—
In aggregate will travel millions of kilometers, yet not move a
Lot from this spot, this hillock. I see them slither here. Surprise!
I'm like a hollow horsetail plant.[15] Clamped on my head an icy vise.
Aagghh! I could read a book, think, reminisce, but I decide I'm—looking.
I quick forget the hare invasion, apples,
                    people, all that's local.

What's quivering in the sky above the forest and below the sun?

What's with provincial places where transcendent women make clouds run?
I see the female spine, see belly-button, down below the loop
Of gold, the distant acid upon which life will cleverly clamp
Like clothespin-chromosomes on a line—X, Y, now they're unfastened,
                                    dragging
A simile for your sanity, empty duvet cover—our will, Lord, is fragile.
That braid, that double helix forms the souls that run in raincoats.
Boy-oxygen and girl-glucose are being clothed in dragonfly paincoats.

Глава вторая. Битва

2.1.

Всё отзывается, хотя бы по третьему правилу Ньютона,

                                        пусть неохотно,
как Одиссей, увидавший семью свою; в землю входящая

                                        плотно,
лопата кидает пласт книзу лицом, огороднику это

                                        во благо,
череп я нахожу, у него в челюстях кляп

                                        из чужого флага.
Пётр, град его вечный и тусклый — окошко, заклеенное

                                        газетой;
гетман обеих сторон Днепра запорожского войска

                                        Мазепа;
его крестница Марфа — ведьмачка с чёрно-бурым румянцем

                                        на скулах;
Карл — рано лысеющий юноша, альфа-омега, Швеция, ваших

                                        загулов,
крепостной гарнизон, воеводы, солдаты обеих держав, пришедших

                                        к позору, к победе, —
я припомню их всех, через полтавское поле сверкая

                                        на велосипеде.

Chapter Two, The Battle

2.1.

Everything responds, at least to Newton's third law,
                                        reluctantly,
Like Odysseus, absent an era, returning delays seeing his
                                        family.
My shovel plunges into the mud with bravado, and what began with gardening
                                                work
Becomes archaeology when a skull with a gag of a stranger's flag is what I
                                                unearth.
Great Peter[16] in Rus, his new town already eternal, window-to-west glued
                                        over by newspapers,
Mazepa, the treacherous Hetman of the Zaporozhtsy on both banks of
                                        Dnieper;[17]
His goddaughter Marfa—the witch who wears black-brown blush
                                                on her cheekbones;
Charles twelfth,[18] Carolus Rex, balding at twenty, invading Swede leader with
                                        alpha-male speech tones;
And you fortress garrison, commanders and soldiers of what would be a nation,
                                        plucking victory from shame—:
As I'm riding my bike through that battlefield, all these I remember and the
                                                most egregious I name.

Вижу: копьё разбивает солдату лицо, вынимая из-под верхних зубов

бездну.

Слышу: вой электрички, подруливаю

к переезду,

миную хозяйство вокзальное, клинику скорби, шоссе — везде

долгий путь,

наконец — огород, в нём лопата торчит, землю пробуя

перевернуть.

Пейзаж перепрятывал время, а время перепрятывало человека:

стоп!

Тормозима надеждой, сабля сыплется над головой,

как верёвочный трап.

Кого пополам развалили, душой открывает шоссе, уходящее

клином на Гадяч,

вот рыцарь помпезный, рогаткой двоясь, меж машинами

скачет,

неискореним был боец, но увидел в автобусе панну и мчится

потрогать —

за лошадиную морду он принимает на поручне согнутый

локоть,

и рухнул долой офицер, драгоценный драгун, и подняться

не может,

а лошадь

ноги забрасывает на солнце лямками сумки

через плечо.

Кто мог погибать по три раза, по три раза погиб,

и погиб бы ещё и ещё.

Куда же вы, шведы?[3] На месте больничного корпуса с надписью

«психиатрия»

они умирали, сражаясь с людьми, по чьим лицам мазнула

стихия,

I see: spear smashes a soldier's face, removing from under the upper teeth

                                              the abyss.

I hear: howl of the elektrichka train[19] and I steer toward a lift-gate on the tracks

                                                  where I cross.

And finally—my garden where a shovel stands up trying to turn the earth's

                                                  resistances.

This landscape concealed spent time and time concealed living persons:

                                                  Stop!—

The saber disassembles above an enemy head, abolishing one man's

                                            particular hope,

Like a rope ladder this soldier ascends, but leaving to witnesses his dead

                                            body intact.

Some of the war dead dispersed, but this one's spirit suffuses our highway

                                            toward Hadyach.[20]

So here's the distributed knight, cut in two parts by a slung shot, and he's

                        horseback between highway cars galloping;

Unkillable warrior who saw in a bus and is racing to touch a lady

                                      and follow her.

Control the horse by the straps on its long narrow jaw with the bit in it,

                                          he thought,

But down he slammed, that precious dragoon, he tried to float up

                                      but could not,

And meanwhile his horse threw its legs, like woman's purse-straps over her

                            shoulder, toward the sun.

Those who could perish three times three times perished,

                                  and would perish again

                                              and again.

Where are you going, Swedes?[21] (Said actually Charles to his retreating men.)

                                      That was here on

The site of the psych hospital. Swedes were dying, dying fighting us,

                              their own brown smeared on

дрались пациенты — о, скважины вырванной мысли! — трубили

и кисли,

на огородных работах бордовый бурак бинтовали,

целуя.

Кто пал на складе железнодорожном, тот встал, словно взрыв

из-под штабеля шпал.

Ты, начавший ещё при Петре, муравей, через поле твоё странствие

длится!

В гуще боя я б мог продержаться не долее вечности, загодяемой

блицем,

в гуще боя я на раскладушке лежал бы в наушниках музыки мира

под абрикосой.

Перепрячет ли время меня? Переправа. Наушники — мостик

над Ворсклой.

Кто б из рыб проскользнул меж сапог, и копыт, и обозных

колёс?

Так запуталась местность летучая в армиях, в прядях

волос.

Ты, кристальная бабочка, разве не будешь изрублена

саблями битвы?

Проще в щелчке фотозатвора порхать, чтоб выйти, подобно

клятве

войска: всезернием запечатляя верность сиятельству

света.

Поле, что тебе свары? Русские — мак и полынь, дрок и васильки —

шведы.

Это поле мой сад вытесняет на небо, фокусируясь в бедной моей

лачуге,

комары надо мною разломом гранита зернятся, морочат свечу,

и —

это поле казалось мне центром планеты, вдруг всплывшим

наружу,

кулаком серебристым, сжимающим точку, откуда исходит

оружие.

Their faces, and fighting now the mental patients—O slits cut into thought!—
This the collapse of time. This from my garden as I bandage, then kiss,

a burgundy beet.

Who is it fell at the railroad and went up exploded with crossties, as then

and now meet?

You, ant, having started way back under Peter the Great, through your field the

journey continues!

In the midst of the battle I'd last no more than an eternity, naked, by cannon

unsinewed.

In the midst of the battle I'd lounge, world music in headphones, beneath the

apricot tree,

With my hearing my crossing, my headphones a bridge over Vorskla.

But can I hide in history?

Who, nobody? would wriggle fish-like between boots, hooves, and

wagons of war?

Armies are tangled with themselves and terrain, stuck-in like locks of hair.
You, butterfly jewel, won't you be cut out of air by

battle sabers?

Easier for you to flutter in the snap shutter of a camera, than me

to record a gabby

Soldier's oath: the animal eye captures our loyalty to the excellence

of light.

Field: past argument. Russians—poppies, mugworts, gorse, cornflowers[22]—

Swedes.

This field surrounds my garden to the sky, my poor cabin the focus of

the site,

Mosquitoes above my head like mica chips unfazed by candles,

and this reads

To me as at the planet's center a compression exploding outwards

as a conception

Of a silver fist, retracting into the magma, only to surface again

as a weapon.

2.2. Точка зрения обозревателя

Сколько однообразья в солдатах, когда их полки объезжают

царь и король!
Все хотели понравиться этой войне, все сияли, но кто же герой?
Отделяется он от рядов, сцепленных так, что ни трусов там нет,

ни героев,
как, сойдя со стены, трепеща и прямясь, уплыла бы полоска обоев.

2.2. Point of View of the Observer

So much of sameness in those soldiers, when regiments process past
                                                            Tsar and King!
They all would have war love them, all would shine, but who did one heroic thing?
An onlooker detaches from these ranks: no cowards and no heroes,
                                                            no pure type,
As if there peels off from a wall fluttering and straightening out a wallpaper stripe.

2.3. Карл

На восьми туманах-гвардейцах над битвой в коляске несомый
                                                        король
покачивается между пуль и в музыку боя впивается, словно
                                                        спираль.
Карл, не будь у тебя ни врагов, ни армад, а только деньги
                                                        и деньги,
ты не спал бы величеством тела на величестве пляжа,
                                                а в деревеньке
рыбацкой нанял бы десятерых, чтобы дрались против тебя и
                                                        скуки,
от твоего лучезарного идиотизма ослеп Мазепа
                                                и его казаки,
если жмурился ты, шли навстречу короны каркасами
                                                радиолярий,
но простейшие не объяснят генералам, где знамёна полки
                                                растеряли,
воевать — это тебе не зайцев стрелять в сейме, прости, излагаю
                                                вольно,
это тебе не стёкла побить с друзьями в лучших домах
                                                Стокгольма.
Я бы создал вам землю вторую, но материалов хватит
                                                на небольшой шар
диаметром около метра; военные на него ложатся в скафандрах,
                                                дыша
из одного баллона, и друг друга гоняют по законам, оговорённым
                                                ООН,

2.3. Charles XII

Foot-shot and carried above the battle by guardsmen in his carriage,

                                     Carolus Rex

Sashays between the bullets and absorbs the melodies of war, as in

                                a spiral nexus.

Charles, if you had no enemies, no armies, but only money

                          and money,

You wouldn't sleep majestically on a majestic beach but

                             in a fisherman's puny

Village, where you'd hire ten to fight you as you fight being

                          bored.

Your brilliant idiocy has blinded Ivan Mazepa and his

                        Cossack horde.

Squint at the light, your own crown advances at you

                      past carcasses of radiolarians.[23]

How explain to your generals the lost banners of regiments are now

                         like protozoa skeletons?

I'm telling you freely, sorry, that to fight a battle: not shooting hares

                      in the sejm[24] in Poland;

And not shattering windows with friends in the best houses of

                      Stockholm.

You deserve another earth, but only enough materials exist

                      for a small sphere,

Diameter one meter; soldiers lay on it in space

                gear.

They're sucking oxygen from one tank and chasing each other in

                    accord with UN decrees.

переползая, словно чулок по лампочке, когда его штопают

со всех сторон.

Вот спугнул офицер офицера и на челе у того сосчитал капельки

пота,

это, значит, разбита в таком-то районе такая-то, скажем,

пехота.

Нет, тебе нравится ездить с оружием и помрачать бесконечности

русских окраин,

нравится, если: а) колют, б) рубят, в) режут мне нравится

шведский дизайн;

думаю, Карл, от признаний моих ты бы впал в драгоценную

ярость:

город для пыток меня ты в ответ основал бы и не ощутил бы

усталость.

Здесь я, фью-фью, что искать и ветвистою злобой морочить

астрал?

Королю наливают стакан, я его осушаю, и меня не ведут

на расстрел;

вот я бью короля по щеке, и король подставляет другую —

не видит меня,

ждёт его допельклепер лифляндский под турецким седлом —

я рассёдлываю коня,

я ладонью полполя королю закрываю, где солдат Авраам[4] похищает

шведское знамя, —

Карл не в силах меня наказать — мёртвые не управляют

нами.

Мёртвые ходят в одеждах из яблочных шкурок на воздухе

летнем, —

лишь вещества! — а историю сделает тот, кто родится

последним.

And up they crawl like a stocking over a light-bulb being darned up
>> by degrees.
An officer frightened another officer, then counted fear's forehead's drops
>> of sweat.
That symbolizes a certain loss in a certain region, let's say an infantry
>> retreat.
No, Charles, you like to shove round your cannons, strike fear
>> in Russian lines,
And you like it if: a) stabbing, b) slashing, c) cutting. For me, I like
>> Swedish designs,
And I like to think, Charles, from my admissions, that you would
>> choke on stored-up rage:
You'd build for me a city of torture and, tirelessly, you'd scissor me,
>> your découpage.
Come get me here, fweet-fweet,[25] and your birdie and your malicious
>> astral bastard?
They pour a drink for you—I drain it, no execution, they're
>> not hasty.
Then I hit king on the cheek king turns the other.
>> I'm invisible.
Here's waiting his Livonian horse, whose crup I strap with saddle
>> from Tunisia.
Obliterate half the field with my hand where Antonov of Nizhni steals
>> the Swedish banner.[26]
Charles lacks the strength to control me. The dead fail always in a
>> fight *mano a mano*.
The dead walk in clothes made of apple peels lifted by summer air of
>> Poltava oblast:
They're beings but bodiless. So history will work exclusively through those who'll
>> be born, oh, last.

Видишь, горки на поле тут и там возникают, оседая

мгновенье спустя, —

это всадники сшиблись, их кони на задних ногах, а передними —

воздух вертя,

осыпается круча, где смерть сердцевину горы вычищает

подкопом

и летит в пустоту человек и уносится неким

потоком.

Кто убит наповал, выпадает из сечи, как батарейка, выкатываясь

из гн езда,

и разряжается в землю, и всходит над Ворсклой неназванная

звезда.

Ты взираешь в трубу золотую, в трубу золотую, в трубу,

ресницы теряя и, увы, интерес,

Карл, на черепе у тебя можно прочесть — дубль-ве! — ты почти уже

лыс!

Кто же поле приподнял с враждебного края, и катится войско на Карла,

и нету заслона?

Стала бессмысленной битва, словно на каждом бойце было написано

Слово.

Есть черепаха на Ворскле, а у черепахи — неприступный

затон,

она похожа на лампу, запаянную в непроницаемо-чёрный

плафон.

С нею нет никого. Ею никто не питается. Её коготь заразен.

Карлу она — друг, брат и сестра — чёрная черепаха с пятиугольным глазом.

See: there appear on the field mounds of horses and men; then
                                                settle down later—
The back legs of horses upended and tangled with two legs
                                                of dead fallen riders.
They whirl in the air. Man-mounds are sinking as death's digging
                                                a hollow mountain below.
Phantasm refocus to the emptiness of men depleted of their
                                                energy flow.
You're killed on the spot, oblit from the battle like a battery removed
                                                from its socket.
Life-power discharges into the ground. An unnamed star then rises over the
                                                Vorskla.
You squint into a golden scope telescope tube, and lose your
                                                eyelashes and your, alas,
Interest, Charles, as you read a—skin-W—on your skull as bald as your
                                                ass!
Who? You! Appropriating this field from enemy land and easily rolling in
                                                your squadrons
For nonsensical warfare, as if tattooing invisible Death on hides
                                                of Swede bodies.
I know a turtle on Vorskla, the river, who nests in a backwater
                                                unreachable, she
Resembles an electrical lamp that has a black lampshade, opaque,
                                                the devotee
Of solitude. No mates. Nobody eats her. Her claw is poisonous. Charles,
Black turtle, pentagonal eye—she's your sister-brother-friend bizarrely.

2.4. Иван Мазепа и Марфа Кочубей

В доме снеди росли, и готовился пир, так распорядился
                                                    Мазепа,
третий день во дворце блюда стояли, и уже менялся
                                                    их запах,
мычали коты от обжорства и неподвижно пересекали залы,
                                                    дичая,
псы задыхались от пищи, под лавками каменели,
                                                    треща хрящами,
рыбы лежали — пока их усыпляли, они подметали хвостами
                                                    двор,
зеркала намокали в пару говяжьих развалов, остывал
                                                    узвар,
тысячи щековин солёных, мочёные губы, галушки из рыбных
                                                    филе,
луфари и умбрины в грибной икре черствели в дворцовой
                                                    мгле;
полк мухобоев караулил еду, и гетман ступал в шароварах,
                                                    как языки,
кривые турецкие вина носили бессонницей трезвые
                                                    казаки,
столь долгоносые мыши, что, казалось, наполовину залезли в кульки,
                                                    алели
бесстрашно на солнце закатном, и, если от них вести
                                                    параллели,
мы наткнёмся на красные перцы в бутылях — так же спокойны
                                                    они;

2.4. Ivan Mazepa and Marfa Kochubey

His castle's full of food and so a feast is ordered by
                           Mazepa.
Third-day-after dishes are smelling up the courtyard, needing
                                   antisepsis,
But luring cats mooing and moving erratic, and dogs getting
                                   anxious,
Overeating to suffocation and cracking their bones while turning to stone
                                   under benches.
Dead fish. While being euthanized they, with their swish tails, could
                                   sweep out the yard.
The masses of dead cow were steaming the mirrors, so it was too hot
                                   to keep cool the uzvar,[27]
Fruit-honey grog. Thousands of salted cheeks, vinegar lips, fish fillet
                                   dumplings,
From bluefish and umbrina,[28] and last of all mushroom caviar culled from the
                                   damp Vorskla swamp.
A regiment of fly-swatters guarded the food. Among his sleepless Cossacks
                                   soaked
In Turkish wine, the Hetman walked in sharovary pants[29]
                                   which looked
Like tongues. The long-nosed field-mice came out of bags and turned
                                   red at sun-set, intrepid.
We stumbled upon what rhymed with red mice, as calm as them, the red
                                   hot peppers
In glass bottles of impetuous vodka, revealed in the blur of leaping
                                   hot red candle flames.

и ещё словно жгучие перцы в стремительной водке, мутились

свечные огни,

и бурели привезённые из Афона лимоны; были настежь

открыты

окна, затянутые холстами, и пышные всюду завиты

рулеты,

и рулетики с хреном, обёрнутые салатным листом, и посуды —

нет им цены! —

и ещё: поглядите, пан гетман, какие занялись вашим домом

цветы!

поглядите, пан гетман, какие цветы ваши очи измором

берут!

Красниус мальвиус роза засовы срывает с тяжёлых

ворот.

Марфа, виновница, имя, в которое вставлена Ф —

буква-мужчина,

медленно входит в хоромы и останавливается смущённо.

Что-то сказал ей Мазепа и смазал её кулаком по уху.

Марфа

прыгнула прямо на гетмана, ступни ее, словно ленточки в небе.

Мазепа

вправо успел уклониться, а левой рукой отбросил противницу.

Марфа

села на корточки у стены и отдыхала, волосы — лимонного цвета.

Мазепа

к ней подошёл и ударил её острым носком по колену.

Марфа

вскочила, и оба, потеряв равновесие, упали и покатились.

Мазепа

In this flicker of flames were browning the brought-from-Atlas[30]
lemons.
The windows wide-thrown to evening were open but covered with curtains
of billowing canvas.
On the tables: everywhere puffed rolls, curly rolls, artisan flake rolls,
big bran rolls,
And best of all pork-with-horseradish roulade rolls wrapped in lettuce leaves—and
the tableware—priceless!
And: Sir Hetman, look at these flowers you've had lackeys place
about the house!
Look, Pan Hetman, at the species of plants you set out to grace with your
aristo sight!
The mallow flower sulks, but red roses rip the bolts from your
heavy gate.
Marfa-for-Mariya, the name adds F to make it
quasi-male,
Goddaughter Marfa slowly enters the castle hall, in fear of self-betrayal.
Something insulting, Mazepa to Marfa, then he smeared her ear with his fist.
Then Marfa
Jumped straight at the Hetman, flashing her foot-soles like steely sky ribbons.
Then Mazepa
Tried dodging right and using his left hand to punch a young female face.
But Marfa
Retreated and rested crouched by the wall, her hair—the color of lemon.
Mazepa
Came over and kicked her, sharp toe on the knee, hetmaniacal boot, so that she,
Marfa,
Jumped up and into him and both lost their balance, fell down and rolled.
Mazepa

бедро ее оседлал и взвыл, задирая искусанное лицо, и покатились:

                                                                снизу
смерть вторую гетман увидел — горящее чучело Чечеля[5] и своё;

                                                         сверху —
крест на ключице у Марфы, который сам подарил ей;

                                                снизу
Марфа увидела росписи на потолке и гетманский подбородок;

                                                сверху —
чучело гетмана над Киевом в светлый день... у Марфы затекает

                                                      рука…
Чучело, словно кит, плывущий хвостом вперёд —

                                          усы торчат из мешка;
это — Иван Степанович, гетман Мазепа, мммаа! — толпа выдыхает —

                                                      паа!...
Тополя пузырятся перед несбывшимся королём Украины;

                                          толпа
имеет голову серной спички, и вот поочерёдно сгорают усы

                                          на скобе,
и мешок оживляется битвой с оранжевым шаром,

                                          нашарив его в себе.
Катится пара дворцом, наконец, расцепились, дрожат, разошлись

                                          по углам,
она спиной повернулась и кровь стирает с лица перед оконным

                                          стеклом.
Мазепа ей говорит: я не ищу себе места в тебе,

                                    уходи!
Крестница кровь стирает с лица, платье разорвано сзади

                                          и на груди,
лопатки ее сближаются так, что мог бы Мазепа их вишенкой

                                          соединить, —

Put a leg high and straddled her hip; then he howled; he lifted her hurt
                                                 face and they rolled. Disrupting
Conscious thought, he saw his own death in the form of his dummy bound
                                                 with the dummy of Chychel,[31]
The traitor; and looking up he saw a cross on Marfa's neck,
                                                 the one which
He gave her. Marfa, looking up, saw a Hetman's chin and a ceiling
                                                 painting—
Was it the Hetman as a dummy over sunny Kiev? . . . Marfa's hand
                                                 feels pained . . .
Was it a dummy like a whale tail-first, propeller-tail,
                                                 whiskery whale?
Yes, him, Hetman Mazepa—Ivan Stepanovich—mmmaa!—him—paa!
                                                 Crowd can now exhale . . .
The world surround will now acknowledge the unfulfilled
                                                 king of Ukraine,
And every head in the crowd's a sulfur match head to burn whale whiskers,
                                                 give him pain.
All this in the frame of the battle, sphere within sphere, a context insane
                                                 will explain.
The he and the she roll round the rooms and finally, trembling, uncouple
                                                 and pass
Into corners where, back turned, she wipes the blood from her face before
                                                 an icon glass.
Mazepa to Marfa: *I want in you no part of me.*
                                                 Get out of here.
Goddaughter blots blood from her face, dress torn down her back and
                                                 off her breast, and where
The blades of her shoulders met, Mazepa could've pressed a cherry
                                                 in there.

несмь доволен Владыко Господи, да внидеши... но тотчас

                                                                      теряет нить, —

несмь доволен Владыко Господи, да внидеши под кров

                                                            души моея,

всякий кусок золота в невесомости принимает форму тела

                                                      ея.

Ввёл он крестницу в спальню, где окна распахнуты

                                                   и пахнет травой,

пол покачнулся под ней, и от испуга вцепилась она в рукоятку

                                                      над головой

и взлетела.

        Пыль оседает пока, мы разберём гордый закон механизма:

гостил у Мазепы однажды инженер из Вероны, пионер

                                                    терроризма,

с фиолетовыми волосами, что-то от барбариса под слабым дождём;

                                                         Мазепе

в доме мечталось давно оборудовать мышеловку для знати;

                                                    трепет

объял инженера, он создал устройство и ускакал возводить

                                                   карусели в Варшаве.

На потолке были два блока из дуба укреплены и свободно

                                                   вращались,

специальный канат был пропущен по блокам,

                                              и с одной стороны

к нему привязали бобовой формы местные валуны,

                                              а с другой стороны

цилиндр, в котором был вырезан паз для упора, дабы не давать

                                                  грузу

увести через блоки канат, но если тянуть его на себя,

                                              сразу

I am not worthy, Lord God, yes, enter[32] . . .—but immediately she loses the thread
$$\text{of the Old Russian prayer.}$$
I am not worthy, Lord God, yes, enter-expand beneath the roof
$$\textit{of my soul.}$$
Thus Marfa whose spirit is weightless, whose body has value the same as
$$\text{her weight in gold.}$$
He pulls his goddaughter into his bedroom; windows are open; the room
$$\text{smells of grass.}$$
She's fragile and fearful. The room sways beneath her. A lever appears and
$$\text{she yanked it: } \textit{volte-face,}$$
By machine she flew up and away. (Parenthesis for story on the laws of this
$$\text{mechanism:}$$
Once Mazepa had a visitor from Verona, engineer, pioneer of
$$\text{terrorism,}$$
Hair purple the color of barberry under light rain. He'd build
$$\text{for Mazepa}$$
A secret escape-chute for nasty nobility; then, too sensitive for Poltava, he'd
$$\text{decamp for}$$
A project in Warsaw to build carousels. The project here was to fix
$$\text{to the ceiling}$$
Two oak blocks holding pulleys that freely revolved, and on
$$\text{these they could thread lengths of unspooling}$$
Rope down to where a person, like Marfa, stood yanking. Counterbalance
$$\text{was got by installing}$$
Above two bean-shaped boulders: these came down when you below stood
$$\text{pulling}$$
The rope through a cylinder. Stones down, you up.
$$\text{Effect immediate . . .)}$$
This the machine that Marfa engaged with the handle, jump-cut to bedroom
$$\text{below her. But wait:}$$

упор вылетал из гнезда, и хитрый канат вверх забирал
                                        машинально,
так и Марфа, дёрнув за рукоятку, была поднята
                                над спальней,
этого мало: место, где стояла она на полу,
                                обратилось в колодец.
Так задумал Мазепа.
                Так исполнил веронец.
Что сказать о колодце, когда он ни звука не возвращал и топил
                                        перспективу?
Легче влезть на стеклянную гору или разговорить полтавскую
                                деву
в угольно-синем белье под оранжевой газовой блузой,
                                оборона во взгляде.
Сколько старшин и полковников Хортицы себя показали
                                на италианском снаряде!
сколько бледнели они — лишь бахрома кумачовых рубцов на лице
                                набрякала,
канули те воеводы, и рукоятка, качаясь, их души вокруг
                                растолкала.
К той рукоятке мясо цепляли, кусища, ну прямо с пирушки
                                пещерной, —
взвейтесь, собачки, и затвердейте от страха, торча,
                                как прищепки!
Марфа летала туда и сюда, каблуки наставляя на гетмана,
                                амплитуда свежела,
вот её вынесло кверху, и воздух она обняла, отпустила
                                и села
гетману прямо на плечи, и он покачнулся, и левой рукой
                                прикоснулся к эфесу,

The place where she stood on the floor had on it a sliding trap
                                                that covered a cistern.
See the idea of Cossack Mazepa, the performed work of the Veronian
                                                master.
Let's draw the veil over the sound-muffling well; it drowns the
                                                perspective.
It's easier to climb a glass mountain, or get a girl from Poltava
                                                to neck, with
Her in her charcoal-blue underwear under an orange-blue blouse,
                                                pretending to sleep.
(I liken to Marfa those Cossack officers on Khortitsa,[33]
                                                island in Dneiper,
Who faced Peter's cannons' projectiles pale-faced but anticipating new
                                                scarlet scars.
Those weapons are gone. Those generals are gone. Their souls are abstractions,
                                                just like their wars.
There once was a machine, it spat out chunks of meat for cave animals
                                                to eat. So feast,
You dogs, on that machine's meat. It's how you eat your fear and so know
                                                you're a beast.)
Return to Marfa, swooping here-there, her heels aimed at Hetman,
                                                increasing the arcs,
She was zooming upwards to apex, hugging the air, then descending
                                                on Hetman she twerks
On his shoulders directly; he staggered; he took his left hand to shape
                                                the hilt of his sword
And felt on his cheeks raw rub of silk stocking, provoking inside him, erotic, a force
Lateral to combat her weight vertical. He summoned a Darwinian starfish—
                                                indeed all extant

и ощутил щеками укол шёлка чулок, побудивший в нём силу, поперечную весу,
силу, берущую в битву полезную Дарвина и морскую звезду, —всех! — помимо
той черепахи (см. предыдущую главку), что с Карлом сравнима.
В мышцах любовников смешана крепость лопастей и небес,
а когда возвратились они, увидали: в тысячах поз
казаки сопели в испарине, разбросанные, словно отрезы

сизого шёлка,

ножки собачек скобкой согнулись, а спинки утрамбовались,

и выросли шейки,

ибо — эволюционировали: с нижних лавок взяли запасы и захотели

с верхних;

торты нетронутые лежали, но башни их повреждены —все в луковых перьях.
и рыбьи скелеты — мел, а головы их — фольга, а в мисках

из-под салата —

уши кабаньи — 6 штук, у него бывает и больше, когда отряхивается

от болота.

У лучших котов концы хвостов раздвоились и умели отщипывать пищу,
мерцали осколки тарелок — были съедены тыщи и не съедены тыщи,
иглицы-птицы, зобы раздувая, клевали столы и пушистые сдобы крошили,
грудились кости обглоданные и дрожали кустиками сухожилий,
были колбасные палки проедены вдоль для забавы, но как —непонятно;
всюду играл холодок, и ловили друг друга по залам, как львы,

бурые пятна;

дух вычитания витал, и торчали ножи, распрямляясь в святой простоте,
по одиночеству с ними сравнимы законы природы,

ярящиеся в пустоте.

Солнце стояло в зените, и ночь во дворце, несмотря на раскрытые ставни,
может, к дверным и оконным проёмам были привалены камни, я допускаю...

Evolution—for battle, excluding—though—that turtle I (last Chapter)
compared to Charles, in my rant.

Now link these lovers-in-combat to battle; love muscles are strong as propellers, as heavens,
So the link is sharp blades, and anyway when lovers looked out they saw
in their poses and positions,

The Cossacks, exhausted, pouring sweat, all scattered, so far away
seeming like swatches

Of blue-gray silk. Phantasmagoria of the after-battle seems as if they're watching
Evolution in acceleration, dog-legs lengthening for spring, dog-backs
Compacted, push out of snouts and visible extension of evolving necks.
Masses of the lower species will take rations from the fewer-richer;
Fish succeed; push down the stacks of cakes—make way for onion shoots
in salad dishes.

Four times more Swedes and Cossacks dead than Russians. Talk not of the dead:
talk food, like ears

Of hogs, six pieces, wash off dirt; like split-tail cats that pinch off their shares.
Animals eating—animals eaten. Thousands eated—thousands uneated. Sometimes
off plates.

The needle-bill birds would puff out their goiters, peck at pastries and accumulates
Of bones already pre-gnawed with strewing of sinews; birds had
scoffed up sausages

Length-wise for sport. Who was it devolved naïve in that chase? How was it
They were now muzzle-blood lions? Spirit of subtraction! Knives out! Holy
simpletons.

The loneliness of Holy Fools[34] a natural law: furiousness[35] of emptiness.
Sun stood at zenith. Night closed on Mazepa's palace, windows and
openings to rooms

All blocked with rocks and choked with traitorous malice, maybe, so I assume.

2.5.

Ни золотой саксофон за плечами, ни мотоцикл, ни брыль с полями...
Ты бредёшь по стране под названием «У», подобная рентгенограмме.
Саксофоны... моторах... навстречу... размазываясь... панораме.

Что за воздух вокруг! Самый тот, что придал человекам носы!
Эти почвы пустили две крепких ноги для Адама степной полосы.
Бритый затылок, свисток из лозы, сиянье бузы и покосы взы-взы.

И создание на смерть ать-два, в оловянных ободьях неся барабаны,
закругляя свой путь и сужая, как панцирь устроен рапаны,
и над конницей в небе не больше, чем школьные парты, парили
                                                                    фарманы.

Но я стал музыкантом, а не адмиралом, работая в сельском баре,
где аграрии пили за любую пылинку, и всем воздалось по вере,
где дельфины в панамках шутили с блондинкой, найденной в море.

А тебя не листали стеклянные двери, молчали на них колокольцы,
и в камнях взволновались мельчайшие волоконцы,
времена сокращая, когда ты в наш бар обогреться.

Ты была, словно вата в воде, отличима по цвету едва от воды,
а мы — оскаленными чернилами вокруг тебя разлиты,
есть мосты, что кидают пролёты в туман, и последний пролёт — это ты.

Я увидел: идёт за тобой неотвязно размахом баталия,
в обороне бароны, и боров на них с бороной, и другие детали...

2.5.

No saxophone slung over shoulder, no motorcycle, no panama
Hat, you wander the "U" country, U-Kraina, roentgenogram of
All sadness. Saxophone . . . engines . . . towards . . . smearing . . . panorama.

What air is around! The very air that gave people noses!
Steppe soils that sprouted two strong legs for people, Adamic resources.
Shaved heads with top-knots—drunk with buza, wheat wine—scythe swath, azz-izz.[36]

There Big Cher created for life, one-two ended in death from the harm in
Its overcooked rods baked in its shell. Here soaring airmen
Looked down on troops looking up, at them in their biplanes called Farmans.[37]

But I: I became a musician, orphic not martial, and I'm working
A village bar. Farmers, drunk with no reason, gain faith from drinking,
And from thinking they see dolphins in panamas, who, with blond mermaids, are
                                                                    joking.

And you: you came easy through silent bar doors, silent you silent bell,
And the stones in the floor speeded geology to swell,
Collapsing time when you entered our warm room to escape a cold-spell.

You[38] were cotton in water, barely distinguishable by color from water,
And we—we vicious ink around you spattered.
There are flights, stairs up through fog: last flight is you, cosmonaut.

What I saw: persistent embattled admirers walking behind you;
And in your defense the harrowers, bishops and hogs that defined you:

Все, теснимые бездной, края твоих юбок топтали.

Разрубленная сорочка. Разрубленная кожа. Разрубленная кость.
Измельченье молекул. О, рознь всласть! Есть
размеры, где жизни нет. Температура окрест 36,6.

Легче делать людей при такой погоде, чем их ломать.
Здесь и там ты расставлена вышками по холмам,
и огранкой твоих повторений охвачена битва — алмаз.

Как тугая причёска без шпильки, рассыпается этот ландшафт,
и на поле другое те же воины валом спешат,
щурятся с непривычки — они из других временных шахт.

Ведь полки могут строиться по вертикали,
повисая в небоскрёбах атак, образуя тающие гантели,
сталкиваясь наобум с теми, с кем ссориться не хотели.

Я узнал в тебе Марфу, носящую семя Мазепье.
Две косицы желты, карандашики словно, изгрызены степью,
только мой саксофон оценил твоё великолепье!

Ты — граница бродячая, всех разделившая стенами, —
водоёмы, леса и пустыни песчинок, сочтённых военными.
Государства лежат между Марфами или Еленами.

Баю-баю, под нашими вишнями дремлешь, колыша гамак,
кровь твою над тобой стёртым зеркальцем крутит комар,
он щекочет радары армад.

You're an abyss, unharmed but your skirt is dirtied in counteroffensive.

Cut shirt. Cut skin. Sawn bones. My girl, you're my image of war.
Disassembly of molecules. O strife as much as we want—or can bear!
Temp now: 36.6. Degrees can be with no life; places no there.

Easier to make people than to break them in this Celsius heat.
Here-there you've set your formations, towers on hills, sharp cut
Repeated diamond designs engulfed by the rush of the battle.

Like a slick hairstyle lacking a bobby pin, this landscape turns into a mess:
Poltava battlefield warriors hurry-scurry *en masse.*
Unused to this they squint—unfixed from their own time, from us.

Dig down regiments, you miners of time, or build up vertically,
Attack hanging from skyscrapers or make of enemy ally,
Colliding randomly with battlefield fellows no longer alien.

You: the girl who doubles as soldier: I now see Marfa in you,
Mazepa-impregnated, pencil-yellow braids, your maidenhood
Steppe-gnawed, and only my sax could sound out your magnitude.

You—you represent borders, dividing us all with partitions and sealing-
Off bodies of water, fragmenting forests and deserts, revealing
A man as a number. You're Marfa, you're Helen of Troy, scene-stealing

As both. Shush-shush. Under our cherries we're napping, hammock's
In motion. Your blood is tempting, ZZZ-ing above you, mosquito.
He's tickling army field-radars with gossip.

2.6. Комар

Ты, комар, звенел в поэме,
в Петербурге, в Вифлееме,
жалил автора «Аморес»,
не жалел свиньи в помоях,
выходи на резкий свет,
сдай поэту свой стилет!

Хором Солнце заслоняя,
как фата, сияет стая,
разворот и —чёрным крапом
вы качаетесь под небом.
Что такое небеси?
Закругленье на скругленье,
точка, тачка без оси.

В комаре ли, в Вавилоне,
свиты тысячи мелодий,
кровь правителя и зека,
лошади и человека,
Лига Наций наш комар,
он — инцест, пунцовый шар!

Вот сидит комар-мечтатель
на виске, как выключатель.
Чин кровавого побора.
Хочет грифелем Памира
на Арктическом щите
написать: я в пустоте.

2.6. Mosquito

You, mosquito, rung bell in the poem,
In Petersburg, in Bethlehem-home,
You who stung the author of *Amores*[39]
Also stung pigs in their forage:
Get over here in bright light or
I'll make you give up you stiletto!

In a choir that blots out the Sun,
Like a veil, the species ascends in chaconne,
Then U-turn—reverse to black specks
Down sky in other direction.
Redefines meaning of sky?
Reversing reversal and why?
Wheelbarrowing, no axis to pivot.

In mosquitos and old cities thrive a
Thousand old songs to jive to.
They mingled the blood of rulers
And convicts, horses/humans, scholars/
Dopes. Each mosquito a League of Nations,
With incest—his vocation.

Here sits the mosquito-dreamer:
Me—switched on—writer and schemer.
Me the foremost donator of blood;
The scribe who'll scrawl, with pencil-lead
From Pamir, on Arctic ice-sheets.
In emptiness I'm the pentathlete.

Ты всему эквивалентен,
ты пустотами несметен,
комарьё с деньгами схоже,
только те — одно и то же.
Облак твой легко умел
строить формы наших тел.

Вы составились в такого…
Полетела ваша лава
над гуляющим Стокгольмом
казаком краеугольным
к северному королю.
Он заглатывал пилю-

лю. А вы перед монархом
вывели своим манером
кровеносную систему,
как разбитая об стену
вдрызг бутылка каберне, —
капля в каждом комаре!

Вы казались человеком
шведу. — Что мне здесь под снегом
чахнуть! — Карл вскрикнул. — Гарвей
опрокинут мощью армий,
есть иные смыслы крови! —
и направился к Полтаве.

You insects are equal to everything;
Not lured to try my every nothing.
Mosquitos—like money just
Identical, based on trust.
Your masses in clouds could mesh
To build the forms of our flesh.

You gathered your swarm back then . . .
Flew densely above the men
Charles Twelve had walking from Stockholm
To join with the cornerstone Cossacks.
Here, Hetman threw in with Charles.
He swallowed the pill of Charles-quarrels.

And you in face of the monarch
Could make the usual plan work.
Circulatory system of blood
Could be tapped, as if we would
Shatter a glass of cabernet esquisito—
One drop sent to each live mosquito!

Why should I wither here under the snow!
Shouted Charles of the north and so
You southern mosquitos were human
Because warm. (Get blood from an army
Otherwise than from warfare, wrote Harvey.)[40]
So come spring Charles fights at Poltava.

Ты, комар, висишь над битвой,
в парикмахерской — над бритвой,
воин, поднятый на пиках, —
на своих ногах великих
над сражением — комар
от ужора умирал.

Умирал, но — обожая
Марфу. Губы освежая —
Марфой. Где она ложится,
в картах чертится граница,
начинается война,
комаровичей весна.

Он за Марфой паром вьётся
в виде что ли пехотинца,
энского полка эпохи
Северной войны. В дороге
по стране с названьем «У»
всё доступно комару.

You, mosquito, you hang above
Their battles, also our barbers whose shave-
Razor drips—spears, razors—your legs
Of power blow battles to rags.
You hang above battle—mosquito.
Blood glutton, dead on the Dnieper.

Were dying, but dying adoring,
Remember *her*, Marfa, imploring
You live with her sexual lips.
Wherever she lays the maps
Have new borders, battles gestate,
And spring mosquitos maturate.

Now he appears in the infantries,
Northern war,[41] Nth regiment, he's
Storing up sting to get Marfa
And he's ZZZing to go to war for
Her, *en route* to a country named U.
To the mosquito all is allowed.

2.7. Медный купорос.
Второе Деловое отступление

Здесь я отдыхаю после похода десятилетнего завоевательного
на пятачке чернозёма в обилии дательного и зевательного,

в небе складками молний трещат хрустальные флаги,
клубни картошки торчат из земли, словно локти из драки;

бултых в океан, ночная страна, срывая времён пояса!
Да, кот забегает ко мне вслед за крысой, а ещё лиса

вслед за крысой, но наперерез коту, а он котам атаман!
Кыш, коллектив зверей! — я в бодрый бью барабан.

Погружу микроскоп в лепесток и окунусь в окуляры,
там, словно в Смутное время в Москве, смерти размеры.

Вот разведу купорос, контролируя лакмусовой бумажкой!
Пешкой кажусь я огромной в балахоне и шлеме, шагая дорожкой.

Сад обливаю, как написано, «до полного смачивания» из шприца.
Уж бирюзовыми стали томаты, черешня и мазанки черепица.

Всё. Жгу отравленные одежды — не употребляемые дважды.
Сад озираю, выкупанный в купоросе, тяжёлый и влажный.

Глухо вокруг, но ненадолго — первыми выключаются мухи
и останавливаются, повсюду себя оставляя звенящими в прахе;

2.7. Copper Framework.
Second Business Retreat

Here I rest in an abundance of dative and yawning—
Rest on a sliver of black earth after a ten-year conquering journey.

In the sky like folds of lightning crackle crystal flags,
Potato tubers protrude from the earth, like in a brawl jagged

Elbows; splash into ocean, night country, secure the link between eras!
At this, here scurries the cat chasing after the rat, also the fox to embarrass

The rat, but fox cuts in front of the cat, but he . . . Chieftain of Cats!
Get out, shoo, you tribe of animals!—I hit the loud drum, stop all that.

Now I twist-focus the microscope onto a petal, dive through the lenses;
See sizes of death, as if in Troubles-in-Thirties Moscovian cleansings.

Well, let's dissolve blue vitriol,[42] and monitor it with a litmus-test strip!
I seem like a chess pawn walking in helmet and hazmat suit, zipped.

Garden-watering, as written, "until fully moistened" by sprayer on hose,
Cherry tree, shingles on hut, tomatoes already turquoise.

All of it. Burning the poison-soaked clothing—no second use.
Observing that garden, vitriol-soaked, damp-heavy with blues.

Surrounding silence, not long. The first to switch off and stop
Are the flies. In dust they give themselves up. Hop, plop, flip-flop and drop.

вновь тишина, а через час валится разом весь колорадский жук
вверх каблуками и оком вощёным защёлкнув последний миг,

следом — личинки — коралловые, живьём не похожие на живых,
пильщики, деревоточцы, стеклянницы — две золотых.

Я же писал тебе: «Есть неорганика в нас, и поэтому
стал я внимательней к собственному устроенью скелетному,

к своеволию мёртвой природы во мне, что роднит меня
с камнем и облаком происхождения метеоритного,

я скажу тебе больше — аж до шевеленья волос —
кристаллизуется в каждом из нас голубой купорос.

Мне одиноко, хоть пёс мой за мною следит, как подсолнух,
нету в округе подобных мне — истинных ли, иллюзорных,

нож заржавел моментально и разломился, как бородинский хлеб,
хлябь разверзлась, и камни вскочили на ноги, чтоб

мне в зрачки заглянуть и шепнуть кости моей: улови,
даже если не через живое, приращенье любви.

Помнишь, на бровке ты голосовала — ночи была середина —
в позе застыв человека, кормящего с пирса дельфина,

помнишь, подъехала тихо машина, и уплотнились поля,
купоросного цвета дельфин её вёл, не касаясь руля...»

The silence is back. In an hour the local squad of Colorado beetles
Falls down fast. Last wink of its waxy eye has slammed shut sweetly.

Next—larvae—the coral, that lives without life's color, like mold;
The sawyers or woodcutters,[43] the glass beetles—last two of these golden.

I wrote to you: "Non-organic matter within us, so
I became more attentive to my skeletal structure, my own bone.

I accept my internal dead nature, which makes me poet laureate
In my families of rocks, and of clouds of meteorological origin.

I'll tell you more—it's bad; your very hairs will quiver—
In each of us blue vitriol crystallizes our liver.

I'm feeling lonely; though my dog does follow me, sunflower to my sun.
Nearby, no one like me, no one likely, i.e., illusioned, no one.

The knife rusted instantly. It crumbled like borodino bread.[44]
The boulders sprung onto the feet; the dirt unfurled; and this led

To your look in my pupils, your whisper to my bones: suffer,
Even if not through the living, augmentation of love.

Remember—on the edge you—were hitching a ride—midnight and you're
Frozen in the pose of a person who feeds a dolphin from the pier,

Remember, quietly a car approached and compacted the fields,
The vitriol-colored dolphin was driving it, not touching the wheel . . ."

Глава третья. Царь награждает

В сознании полтавчан битва не теряет актуальности и в наше время. Эпизоды сражения живо обсуждаются в транспорте, в очередях, на парковых скамеечках. В ностальгических стихах современных баталистов есть стремление повернуть историю вспять, чтобы снова увидеть победителя и побеждённых, ощутить возможность и смысл героизма. Привожу сердечные и несколько неуклюжие строки, появившиеся в газете «Ворскла» от первого июля 1984 года.

А с пьедестала смотрит величаво
сам Пётр, как будто бы живой,
и вспоминает дни военной славы
и памятный полтавский бой...
Нас не одна эпоха разделяет,
а двести семьдесят пять лет.
Здесь перед тобой лежит земля родная,
здесь поле славы и побед.

* * *

Царь сердца осязал конкретно, как доктор Амосов.
Царь наградил небо землёю и наоборот.
Царь утвердил циркуль в груди генерала и очертил полмира.
А тебе — ворону на грудь, ты не подвёл.
Как царица Химия, царь стоял перед ними.
Трубили ангелы в костяные горны.
Царь над героем склонился.
Голову развосьмерил в надраенных пуговицах его.

Chapter Three, The Tsar Rewards

In the consciousness of Poltava residents, the battle does not lose relevance in our moment. Episodes of the battle are vigorously discussed in transport, in lines, on park benches. In nostalgic poems of the modern poet of battle-pieces, is an aspiration to reverse history, to see once again the victor and vanquished, to feel the opportunities and the meaning of heroism. I'll present here the heartfelt and somewhat awkward lines, appearing in the newspaper *Vorskla* on the first day of July of the year 1984:

It's Peter himself up there in bronze,
And looking magnificent, as if alive,
Reminding Rus we had war-glory once,
And Poltava's victory is forever the proof . . .
That was eras and eras and eras ago,
In fact two hundred and seventy years.
You, visitor, your native land below
Is field of thoughts too deep for tears.

* * *

Tsar touched the heart precisely like Dr. Amosov.[45]
Tsar rewarded the sky with the earth and vice versa.
Tsar set up the compass[46] in his general's chest and traced half of the world.
And Tsar had for you—crow on your chest, because you didn't disappoint.
Like Tsarina of Chemistry, Tsar stood before everybody.
Angels trumpeted with horns made of bones.
Tsar bowed over the hero.
Tsar head reflected eight times in Tsar's polished buttons.

На фрейлинах — юбки густые со льдом.

Пряные кавалеры поодаль.

Царь стряхивал с лица невидимые морзянки — лицом.

Казалось, не было у царя рук.

Уже в размере его стопы содержится часть пути.

Царь награждает.

Медали теплели на груди офицеров.

Времяобразование.

Фрейлина вполоборота.

Бывает, у большей рыбы меньшая торчит изо рта.

У царя голова была мала.

Тело ело царя.

Поскольку материя неуничтожима, главное в ней — выносливость.

Не с людьми сражаетесь, а со смертью.

А из бессмертия какую свободу ты вынес?

Если сражаешься ради резона, резоннее сдаться.

1461 пушечный выстрел за пять часов боя, а?

Нева в папоротниках вёсельных лодок.

А паруса — скорлупы выпитых яиц.

Царь награждает.

Отвагу — подобием человека.

Терпение — подобием отваги.

Землю — тенью своей.

Царь награждает.

Перспективу, за то, что удар уточняла, даль сведя воедино.

Камни — геном времён: от камней происходит время.

Царь свинец награждает вниманьем — записывает: свинец.

Смерть! Шведами тебя награждает царь!

Those ladies-in-waiting: skirts thick with ice.
Spicy cavaliers in the distance.
Tsar shook off of his face along with his face invisible letters of Morse code.
Seemed like Tsar had no hands.
Already his foot measures the first part of the journey.
Tsar rewards.
Medals are warming on the chests of officers.
Time of the forming-up of regiments.
Lady-in-Waiting in half-turn.

Sometimes in a larger fish a smaller fish sticks out of its mouth.
Tsar had a small head.
Body ate the Tsar.
Since the material is indestructible, most important thing in it is—endurance.
Not with people you fight but with death.
And: from immortality which freedom did you take away?
If fighting involves reason it is more reasonable to surrender.
1461 firings from cannons during five hours of battle, ay?
Neva River surfaces stirred by paddle boats.
And sails—sails that are the shells of emptied eggs.
Tsar rewards.

Courage—in the likeness of a man.
Patience—in the likeness of courage.
Earth—by one's shadow.
Tsar—rewards.
Perspective, for making cannon-shot precise, jamming distances together in one.
Stones as the genomes of time: from stones begin time.
Tsar rewards metal of bullet lead with his attention; writes down: pencil-lead.
You, Death! Tsar rewards you with Swedes.

Любовников боя — ложем с гипсовыми пружинами, — пусть лежат

неподвижны!

Царь сел перед армиями и стал книгу листать и долго листал.
Где брат мой, Карл?
Как борода на спиннинге — на шляху перепуталась божевольных

толпа.

Здесь ли царь брата искал?
Где брат мой, Карл?
Царь награждает.
Поле ночное в переливах лазутчиков — звездой из 1000 жерл.
Где брат твой, Карл?
Трёх лошадей, под фельдмаршалом раненных, обвенчал святотатец.
Где, Карл, твой братец?
«Побеждающий да не потерпит вреда от смерти второй».
В топких венках — гробы офицеров.

Царь награждает.
Историков — чем попало.
А пленных — обедом.
Военспецам немецким в спецовках царь за ц/у выдал русские деньги.
Мальчишки казнили маршала шведов.
Зеркало подносили к его очкам.
Маршала шведов били палками.
Маршалов пальцы белели.

Награждаются:
Меншиков А. Д.,
Я. В. Брюс,
Шереметьев Б. П.,

Lovers of battle—you get hard beds of plaster springs, so lay there

motionless!

Tsar sat before the army and began to flip through a book and flipped for a long time.
Where is my brother, Charles?
Spinning, spinning—a crazy crowd has mixed themselves

in the road.

Is it amidst this where Tsar looked for the brother?
Where is my brother, Charles?
Tsar rewards.
Night field in iridescence of spies—by star-light from 1000 muzzles of cannons.
Where is your brother, Charles?
Three wounded horses under a field-marshal,[47] married up with blasphemers.
Where is, Charles, your brother?
"The winning one will not tolerate harm from a second death."
In spongy wreaths graves of officers.

Tsar rewards.
Historians—you get whatever.
And prisoners of war—you get lunch.
To German military experts in his uniforms, Tsar for valuable information distributed money.
Boys executed the Swedish marshal.
Mirror brought up to his glasses.
Hit the Swedish marshal with sticks.
Marshal's fingers becoming whiter.

Were rewarded:
Menshikov, A. D.,[48]
J. V. Bruce,
Sheremetev, B. P.,

М. М. Галицин,

Репнин А. И.,

И. И. Скоропадский и др., не вошедшие кадр.

Где брат мой, Карл?

Ему — «камень, и на камне написано новое имя, которого никто...»

Царь награждает.

Царь меня награждает.

Цифры — за то, что они легче времён и не тонут — павшими одушевил.

Крепости коменданта А. С. Келина львом наградил, влитым

в металл.

Фары патрульной машины на повороте сдирают шкуру со льва.

Вечер в Полтаве и во всей Европе.

Сияют фонтаны.

Офицеры выходят из театра.

Бронзовый лев держал в зубах чугунное ядро.

Давно укатилось ядро, но лев не чувствует перемен.

Вид его ужасен.

Следствие не помнит причину.

Царь награждает.

Где брат твой, Карл?

Там, в степи,
шёл твой дубль
на убыль.

Будь поле чисто, как воздух!

Железо, брысь!

M. M. Golitsyn,

Repin, A. I.,

I. I. Skoropadsky and others, names not entered here.

Where is my brother, Charles?

To him—stone. "Stone and on the stone is written a new name, whom no one . . ."

Tsar rewards.

Tsar rewards ME.[49]

Numbers, because they're lighter than time and they don't sink. Brought back to life by soldiers
    who've fallen.

Fortress of Poltava Commandant A. S. Klein is awarded a lion,

                                            cast in metal.

Headlights of the patrolling car, on the turn, rip off the hide from the lion.

Evening in Poltava and in all of Europe.

Shine fountains.

Exit officers from theaters.

The bronze lion held in its teeth the cast iron cannonball.

Rolled away long ago the cannonball, but lion feels no change.

His appearance horrendous.

Consequences don't remember their cause.

Tsar rewards.

Where is your brother, Charles?

There, in the steppe,

You made your turn

To your decline.

Battlefield be clear field, like air!

Battlemetal,[50] get out of here!

Примечания

1   См. памятник Шевченко в Полтаве, автор Кавалеридзе. Он похож на гору летящих друг с дружки тележек, чей суммарный вектор упирается в нуль, и скатиться, поборов мёртвую точку, тележка не может. Смыслы пересекаются и в том, что пушка вводит, а памятник — выводит целые нации из мёртвой точки, — я её называю мушкой, или — во втором случае — чистой гравитацией.
2   Маркс К. Капитал. Партиздат, 1936, т. 1, с. 311.
3   Слова Карла XII, обращённые к отступающим полкам соотечественников.
4   Солдат Нижегородского полка Авраам Иванович Антонов, прокладывая себе дорогу саблей, первым захватил трофей — знамя шведов.
5   Полковник Чечель был в сговоре с изменником и защищал от Меншикова батуринскую ставку. Чучела гетмана и полковника по приказу Петра казнили всенародно в Киеве ещё до полтавского сражения.

1. See the Shevchenko monument in Poltava by the artist Kavaleridze. It looks like a heap of handcarts flying together, whose final vector is held up by nothing, having overcome the dead point, the handcart is unable to run down. Meanings intersect where the canon lets in, but the monument lets entire nations out of the dead point. I call it [the canon] the fire-arm's scope, or pure gravitation.
2. Marx, K.arl. *Capital*, Vol. 1 (Moscow: Partizdat, 1936), 311.
3. The words of Charles XII to the retreating regiments of his countrymen.
4. A soldier of the Nizhny Novgorod regiment, Avram Ivanovich Antonov, paving his way with a saber, was the first to capture a trophy—the banner of the Swedes.
5. Colonel Chechel was in collusion with the traitor and defended Baruryn's headquarters against Menshikov. Effigies of the hetman and the colonel, on the order of Peter, were executed publicly in Kyiv before the battle of Poltava.

Translator's Notes

1. The opening lines have memories of Alexander Pushkin, Alexei Parshchikov's favorite writer: Pushkin had similarly addressed his own talent, and his own writing implements. Also, Pushkin wrote a long poem, *Poltava*, on the 1709 battle and its major named actors—Charles XII, Ivan Mazepa, and Mazepa's goddaughter Marfa Kochubey. There are two other literary references worth noting here, though these are unlikely to have been known to Parshchikov: Lord Byron's long and unreadable poem titled *Mazepa*, and Samuel Johnson's twenty or so immortal and devastating lines on Charles XII in his satire, *The Vanity of Human Wishes*.
2. A string of fish that a fisherman keeps immersed and alive in water.
3. A key of the typewriter's keyboard. The Russian letter *tverdyi znak*, or hard sign, has no sound of its own but is used as an orthographic device.
4. The original refers to Veles/Volos, the Slavic god of earth, waters, cattle, and the underworld. When Christianity took over and followers of paganism were converted, St. Blaise, patron saint of cattle, became the Christian version of Veles to make the assimilation easier.
5. The original uses the term "point of support." One synonym could be "fulcrum."
6. A wagtail is a bird.
7. Referring to the butts of the rifles.
8. The pronoun "her" refers to the point of support.
9. The Vorskla River at Poltava, mentioned again at a few points below.
10. At this point, Alexei Parshchikov has a footnote in prose on the printed page. He writes about a statue of the national poet of Ukraine, Taras Shevchenko, done in constructivist style and placed (decades ago) in the city center of modern Poltava. It looks like a heap of handcarts flying together, whose final vector is held up by nothing; having overcome the dead point, the handcart is unable to roll down. Meanings intersect where the cannon lets in, but the monument lets entire nations out of the dead point. I call it [the cannon] the fire-arm's scope, or pure gravitation." This is obscure, but some help is gained by looking up Ivan Kavaleridze on the internet and seeing there the images of his statue.
11. Mali Budyshcha is a village in the Poltava *oblast* or region.
12. Karl Marx apparently said something like this in part one of *Capital*; the term "donkey" is our substitution for the original's Russian for "horse."
13. Here the translator is tempted to introduce the names Cain and Abel, by way of explanation, but the original does not name the shepherd brothers. Slightly below, the translation gives in to this temptation.
14. In Russia, the day of celebration of the 1917 revolution.
15. In the original, the Russian has "this is a horsetail feeling." The horsetail is a non-flowering plant with a hollow jointed stem.

16 Peter the Great is the Russian tsar who reigned from 1682 to 1725.

17 Hetman is a political title from Central and Eastern Europe, applied to military commanders. The Zaporozhtsy lived beyond the Dnieper Rapids, in lands located in today's central Ukraine. Ivan Stepanovych Mazepa is the full name of the leader of the Cossacks.

18 Charles XII was king of Sweden from 1697 to 1718.

19 The *elektrichka* is a multiple-unit train, consisting of self-propelled carriages; it runs by electricity.

20 Hadyach is a city in Ukraine.

21 Words of Charles XII, directed to his retreating regiments.

22 The poem's many references to plants and animals show the author's training as an agronomist, and also are a primary evidence that in his work he's using ecology to think about history in one particular patch of Ukraine.

23 Radiolarians are protozoa of tiny diameter, which produce intricate mineral skeletons, typically with a central capsule dividing the cell into inner and outer portions of endoplasm and ectoplasm.

24 The Sejm is the lower house of Parliament in Poland.

25 "Fweet-Fweet" are mocking sounds of bird-song.

26 A soldier from the Nizhny Novgorod regiment, Abraham Ivanovich Antonov, cutting his way through with a saber, was the first to capture the trophy of a Swedish banner.

27 *Uzvar* is a traditional Ukrainian drink, prepared from dried fruits sweetened with honey or sugar.

28 These are types of fish.

29 Traditional Ukrainian sharovary trousers, for dancing, are fitted at the waist with a long sash. Their fine fabric balloons out from thigh to knee and is then tightly fitted for tucking into boots.

30 Mount Athos: mountain and peninsula in northeastern Greece; important center of Eastern Orthodox monasticism.

31 Colonel Chychel was a member of Mazepa's conspiracy against Peter the Great. Just below: on the order of Peter the Great, dummy figures of Chychel and Mazepa were mock-executed in Kiev before the battle of Poltava.

32 These are the words of the Second Path of the Holy Eucharist, an old prayer; the original has these words, here italicized, in Old Russian spellings. In this context, the reference to the prayer is very likely blasphemy.

33 Khortitsa is a large island in the Dnieper River, where the Zaphoroztsy built a stronghold (called by them a Sich).

34 The Holy Fools are a type of character in Russian lore: naïve, unsophisticated, and trusting persons. Alexandra Smith suggests the poet in two places considers himself a Holy Fool. See her excellent account of the Poltava poem in Alexandra Smith, *Montaging Pushkin: Pushkin and Versions of Modernity in Russian Twentieth-Century Poetry* (Amsterdam and New York: Rodopi, 2006), 321.

35 The original Russian certainly means "furious" but can also mean "in heat," as in estrus.

36 Imitating the swishing sound of the scythe.

37 This refers to a kind of biplane created by a French plane-designer called Farman. Two anachronisms added in the translation, and not in the original, are the verb "twerks" above and, here in this tercet, the reference to the disaster at the Chernobyl nuclear plant. The date of the Chernobyl event is 1986, one year after the first publication of this poem.

38 The feminine singular form is used in the Russian original. "You" is a woman.

39 The poet who wrote *Amores* is Ovid.

40 William Harvey, a seventeenth-century English physician, was the first to describe in detail the circulation of blood in the human body.

41 This, over time, became the general term for the conflict in which a coalition led by the tsar of Russia successfully contested the Swedish Empire in Northern, Central, and Eastern Europe.

42 Vitriol is sulfuric acid; the chemical composition is $CuSO_4$.

43 "Woodcutters" is a non-scientific name for these beetles.

44 This is dark brown sourdough rye bread, of Russian origin.

45 Nikolai Mikhailovich Amosov was a Soviet and Ukrainian doctor of Russian origin. He was a heart surgeon, known for his inventions of several surgical procedures for treating heart defects.

46 Compass: meant literally as the tool used to draw circles.

47 Field-marshal: a very senior military rank.

48 The six people who were rewarded are Prince Menshikov, a Russian statesman, friend of Peter, and the *de facto* ruler of Russia for two years; Count Bruce, a statesman, general, diplomat, and scientist, one of Peter's chief associates; Count Sheremetev, a: Russian diplomat and general field-marshal during the Great Northern War; Prince Golitsyn, a Russian field-marshal, later also governor of Finland; Prince Repin, a Russian general during the Great Northern War; and Skoropadsky, the Ukrainian hetman of the Zaporozhtsy, the successor of Ivan Mazepa in that role.

49 In the Russian original, the personal pronoun "me" is in regular font, but here it is made larger for emphasis, so that the Tsar-poet relation is not lost. Chapter three triangulates the three Ps: Peter, poet, Poltava. Chapters one and two are in the mode of Pushkinian insouciance, but in chapter three the writer, with abruptly non-metrical lines equal to sentences, must angrily formulate his relation to Peter the Great as one of ambiguous reward. Peter must be faced last and in a different way than Charles XII and Mazepa. The new business of chapter three is to inquire how it is that a dynastic tyrant in Russia, from centuries ago, can reward a person writing in the twentieth-century Soviet state. After all, tyrants require, and know how to attach to themselves, enablers; in the poem, aside from the speaker, the other enablers are aristocratic warriors and contemporaries of the tsar. Here, perhaps, the heritage of the Victor of Poltava is the historical ambiguity and contention in the narrative itself of the *poema*. There is the very particular vexed inheritance of a person from and in Ukraine writing in Russian.

50 Colloquially, the original Russian has: "Metal, shoo!" We may suppose the speaker is reacting against finding in his field centuries-old chunks of cannons and knives. These, like his poem, are what might remain, might remind. The poem's ending lines perform a quick re-framing of the action. The clear air of history, and of natural history in the form of gardens, has its role in making all battles, tyrants, and dynasties eventually seem ridiculous.

Photographs

1. Leningrad. Fall 1988.
Left to Right: Robert Creeley,
AP, Misha Khazin, Arkadii
Dragomoshchenko
(American poet Creeley was
giving a formal reading at a
palace on Nevsky Prospect)

2. Leningrad.
Fall 1988.
AP in the center
of photo

3. Leningrad. Fall 1988.
Arkadii
Dragomoshchenko
and AP

4. Moscow.
Fall 1988.
Dmitri Prigov and
AP in Prigov's
apartment

5. Kyiv.
Fall 1988.
AP from behind;
man on right is
Yurii Mezenko

6. Kyiv.
Fall 1988. Yurii
Mezenko and AP
outdoors

7. Kyiv.
Fall 1988.
AP and Yurii
Mezenko

Printed in the USA
CPSIA information can be obtained
at www.ICGtesting.com
JSHW050046221123
52504JS00007B/41